I believe Ted Haggard's book  fresh and compelling insight all. God has blessed Ted with things simple and simple thing~

—Mike Bickle
Director, International House of Prayer
Kansas City, Missouri

Ted Haggard's witness is inspiring. Against the odds, regardless of the challenges, he helps us see the primary purpose for living. Invest in yourself. Enrich a life. Read this book.

—Bishop Charles E. Blake
Minister, West Angeles Church of God in Christ
Los Angeles, California

As I have had the opportunity to observe Ted Haggard up close over the past three years, what has been clear is "this guy is for real." This book contains principles that are "for real." Reading it will encourage you, challenge you, and make you a believer that all is not lost in the church or the city. More than that, the truths contained in *Your Primary Purpose* are transferable to any church in any city of the world.

—Luis Bush
International Director,
AD2000 and Beyond Movement
Colorado Springs, Colorado

It's time to reach out to our communities and cities with the love and grace of Jesus Christ. Pastor Ted Haggard has been used of God in an extraordinary way to do just that. This book is filled with inspirational and practical insights on how we can minister to our communities. I encourage you to read it prayerfully and expectantly.

—Dr. Paul Cedar
Chairman and CEO, Mission America Coalition
Palm Desert, California

Ted has written a powerful book desperately needed in this hour. It is about *people*—who need help. It is about *passion*—the love God has put in us. It is about *prayer*—getting in touch with God in a personal way. It is a *plan* for action—specific instructions on making a difference right now in the world where we live.

—BILLY JOE DAUGHERTY
PASTOR, VICTORY CHRISTIAN CENTER
TULSA, OKLAHOMA

Ted Haggard's *Your Primary Purpose* contains more practical insights on how believers can impact their communities for Christ than any other book I've read. If you've prayed for practical steps to help see your community's spiritual climate change, *Your Primary Purpose* could well be the answer to that prayer.

—DICK EASTMAN
INTERNATIONAL PRESIDENT, EVERY HOME FOR CHRIST
COLORADO SPRINGS, COLORADO

Reading Pastor Haggard's book helped me greatly to see more clearly how different we are in our approach to interpreting events and influences in our city. This leads me all the more to thank God for our friendship and mutual respect. By "concentrating on the absolutes," as he says, we are able to pray together and seek the Holy Spirit's wonderful works in our community as brothers in faith.

—RETIRED BISHOP RICHARD D. HANIFEN
BISHOP OF THE CATHOLIC DIOCESE OF COLORADO SPRINGS

In my perspective, Ted Haggard is one of today's top ten rising spiritual leaders, a key man whose humility and practical yet sensitive style continue to cause me to want to listen to what Jesus is saying through him.

—JACK HAYFORD
FOUNDING PASTOR, THE CHURCH ON THE WAY
VAN NUYS, CALIFORNIA

Your Primary Purpose is one of the best how-to books I have ever read on how to change a city's spiritual climate. Pastor Haggard describes the Christian's primary purpose as that of making it hard for anyone to go to hell from our home towns, and then gives us basic, biblical guidelines to accomplish that mission.

Throughout the book, he also highlights our Christian responsibility as one of praying for our cities as though it were a life-and-death matter—because it is! And by showing us how to engage in servant-minded spiritual warfare, he demonstrates how we can effectively communicate God's timeless message in a changing world to the glory of God.

—MARILYN HICKEY
MARILYN HICKEY MINISTRIES
DENVER, COLORADO

Colorado Springs has not been the same since Ted Haggard came to town. Its spiritual atmosphere has been charged by the strategies God has placed in Ted's heart. Here is a pastor who builds up all the other pastors in his city. Their unity has made Colorado Springs a spiritual lightning rod.

—TERRY LAW
WORLD COMPASSION/TERRY LAW MINISTRIES
TULSA, OKLAHOMA

Ted Haggard—probably more than any other pastor I know—has a vision that embraces a whole city, not just a local church. Until I read his book *Your Primary Purpose*, I wasn't fully aware of the impact his vision has made on the city of Colorado Springs. The results are absolutely phenomenal. You can be sure, this book is not just spiritual hype, but contains real, grassroots principles that, when applied, will work for any church in any community.

—DON MEARES
SENIOR PASTOR, EVANGEL CHURCH
UPPER MARLBORO, MARYLAND

Your Primary Purpose presents power-packed, practical principles that provide the impetus for change in the spiritual, social, cultural, and economic environment in our cities, towns, and nations. I would highly recommend this work to all serious students of the Word of God and to every Christian leader desiring not just to maintain the status quo in his city, but also to impact his society with the view to bringing generational transformation in his context.

—DR. MYLES MUNROE
PRESIDENT, BAHAMAS FAITH MINISTRIES, INTERNATIONAL
NASSAU, BAHAMAS

Given the recent explosive interest in church growth and spiritual warfare, it's nice to have someone remind us why it makes so much sense to pursue these activities. While strategy and methodology are important—and this book offers plenty of both—*Your Primary Purpose* is ultimately about rationales. And it should be. For if Ted Haggard's own experience tells us anything, it is that true success (the kind that lasts) must flow from a deep understanding of *why* we are doing what we are doing.

—GEORGE OTIS JR.
CEO, FOUNDER AND PRESIDENT, THE SENTINEL GROUP
LYNWOOD, WASHINGTON

I have pastored alongside and have known Ted and Gayle Haggard for fifteen years. Their wisdom, integrity, and compassion for the lost were pivotal in the radical transformation of Colorado Springs. *Your Primary Purpose* shows believers how to demolish every "high thought" so that our churches can pray, unite, and harvest together.

—LARRY STOCKSTILL
SENIOR PASTOR, BETHANY WORLD PRAYER CENTER
BAKER, LOUISIANA

Colorado Springs is not the same city that it was a few years ago. Families are drawn to a new gold rush of family values and spiritual peace in the community. Legislation did not make it possible, but a concentrated effort of local churches did. As a pastor, Ted's new book *Your Primary Purpose* inspires me to do more in my city. I know it will do the same for you.

—BOB YANDIAN
PASTOR, GRACE FELLOWSHIP
TULSA, OKLAHOMA

YOUR
PRIMARY
PURPOSE

YOUR
PRIMARY
PURPOSE

TED HAGGARD

Charisma
HOUSE
A STRANG COMPANY

Most STRANG COMMUNICATIONS/CHARISMA HOUSE/SILOAM/FRONTLINE/ REALMS products are available at special quantity discounts for bulk purchase for sales promotions, premiums, fund-raising, and educational needs. For details, write Strang Communications/Charisma House/Siloam/Front-Line/Realms, 600 Rinehart Road, Lake Mary, Florida 32746, or telephone (407) 333-0600.

YOUR PRIMARY PURPOSE by Ted Haggard
Published by Charisma House
A Strang Company
600 Rinehart Road
Lake Mary, Florida 32746
www.charismahouse.com

Unless otherwise noted, all Scripture quotations are from the Holy Bible, New International Version. Copyright © 1973, 1978, 1984, International Bible Society. Used by permission.

Scripture quotations marked KJV are from the King James Version of the Bible.

Scripture quotations marked NKJV are from the New King James Version of the Bible. Copyright © 1979, 1980, 1982 by Thomas Nelson Inc., publishers. Used by permission.

Cover design by Judith McKittrick

First Edition, 1995
Revised Edition, 2006

Library of Congress Cataloging-in-Publication Data
Haggard, Ted.
Your primary purpose / Ted Haggard.-- [Rev. ed.].
    p. cm.
ISBN 1-59185-623-X (pbk.)
1. City missions. 2. Mission of the church. 3. City churches. 4. City
clergy. 5. Colorado Springs (Colo.)--Church history. I. Title.

BV2653.H34 2005
269'.2--dc22
                                2005013210

Portions of this book were previously published in the first edition as *Primary Purpose*, copyright © 1995 by Charisma House, ISBN 0-88419-381-0.

06 07 08 09 10 — 987654321
Printed in the United States of America

DEDICATION

I OWE MANY OF the principles in this book to the influence of a great man, Pastor Roy Stockstill (affectionately known as Brother Roy) of Bethany World Prayer Center in Baker, Louisiana.

The first time I met Brother Roy, I had driven up to Bethany to make an appointment with him. As I pulled into the parking lot, I noticed a man off to one side painting a fence. I stopped to ask him where I might find Pastor Roy Stockstill. He looked at me politely and said, "I am Roy Stockstill. May I help you?"

I was surprised, but I knew I needed to set up an appointment with him, so I said, "What do I need to do to set up an appointment with you?"

He looked at me and replied graciously, as only a southern brother can, "If you would like, you may set up an appointment with me by picking up a paintbrush and helping me paint this fence."

By watching Brother Roy's life, I learned many of the philosophies that make ministry a pleasure. Though many experienced pastors become tired, cynical, bitter, or weary, Brother Roy found a series of secrets in ministry that cause him to be faithful, fun, life giving, and steadfast. His wisdom and keen insight cause those who are just beginning in ministry, and those who have been extremely effective for the cause of Christ, to desire his counsel and prayers.

I believe God sovereignly placed me in a position to observe and learn from Brother Roy, and those lessons have paved the way for steady ministry for me.

To this honorable man of God I humbly dedicate this work, knowing that his wisdom far surpasses the quality of ideas written here.

Toward the autumn years of my life, should God grant me the years of positive influence He has given Brother Roy, I would be very grateful.

ACKNOWLEDGMENTS

S PECIAL THANKS TO those who labored together with me on this book.

First to my wife, Gayle, for her invaluable assistance in writing, editing, and late-night rearranging. And to our very patient five children who heard about this book during birthday parties, picnics, baseball games, chores in the stables, Thanksgiving and Christmas celebrations, and every other family event for six months.

In addition I want to thank the wonderful people from New Life Church who encouraged me to write this book and allowed me to neglect returning their phone calls, cancel office appointments, and miss weddings and funerals in order to complete it.

And to our exceptional church staff who, under the competent leadership of Lance Coles, came to me and said they would assume additional responsibilities so I, Meg Britton (secretary), and Ross Parsley (associate pastor) could work as a team on this project. All of these friends sacrificed in order to allow the production of this book. Thank you.

And finally, a heartfelt thank you to my parents, the late Dr. J. Marcus and Rachel Haggard, who instilled fundamental values and an appreciation for genuine godliness in me. Without their influence this book would have been impossible. Thank you.

CONTENTS

RETURNING TO OUR PRIMARY PURPOSE

OUR BOOKSHELVES ARE full of Christian books and videos. We have churches on every major street with more staff people than ever before, large Sunday school departments, cell group systems, and megachurch seminars. We have Christian bumper stickers, political action groups, huge parachurch ministries, and extensive social programs. We have built huge churches, ministries, universities, and homes—and in the midst of it all, we are not adequately impacting our culture.

We have beautiful seminaries, wonderful libraries, and scholarly theological analysis. People in some churches are laughing, resting in the Spirit, and vigorously interceding. Other churches are tired, broke, and bitter. Our own television, radio, and literature campaigns make us believe that we are making a difference. And our prophets tell us that we are—but the statistics don't.

It's time for a levelheaded, Spirit-dominated, Bible-based return to our primary purpose. It can be done. This book provides the proof.

- Section I explains our purpose and the opportunities of our generation working through the local church to impact cities.

- Section II reveals five proven principles that can be used anywhere to cause the body of Christ to be more effective.

- Section III stresses biblical virtues and teachings that are necessary to make the five principles work—I call them "lifestyle warfare."

- The conclusion is the charge: we are the ones equipped and responsible for making a difference. And changing our cities is not only possible, but it is also easy (and natural for us as Christians).

—ONE—

OUR PURPOSE,
OUR OPPORTUNITY

MY PHONE WOULD not stop ringing. I was answering call after call and letting others go straight to voice mail. It felt as if the whole day had been this way, and it wasn't yet noon! Frustration was setting in. I had been speaking at a pastors' conference in Baltimore, Maryland, and several projects back home in Colorado needed immediate attention. I am usually patient through busyness, but the morning had been particularly draining, and I had to catch myself to make sure I did not snap at the person on the other end as I said hello.

"Hello, this is Ted."

It was my assistant. "Pastor Ted, Prime Minister Ariel Sharon wants a handful of evangelical leaders to meet with him right away. We received his invitation today, and I wanted you to know as soon as possible."

I stopped in my tracks. What did the prime minister of Israel want with me?

As it turned out, a team of American representatives would be meeting with Prime Minister Sharon to discuss American views on the State of Israel. Sharon knew that American evangelicals constitute some of Israel's most avid supporters, and he wanted to make sure that our voices were heard in the ongoing discussion about Israeli policies. The political importance was obvious to me, but still, it was an incredible moment. I was raised on a pig farm! I grew up in a modest town in the Midwest! And now the State of Israel wanted to fly me to the Middle East to meet with the prime minister.

It was not the only time in recent memory that I had been stopped in my tracks. Opportunities to speak with heads of nations and major figures in politics, finance, and the media had been—and still are from time to time—cropping up. In the last few years, evangelical Christians have been garnering a great deal of public attention. The issues that are closest to our hearts—protecting the weak (including the unborn), defending sacred institutions such as marriage, and advocating religious freedom for people all over the world—are front and center in national and international politics right now, and our perspective is being sought on a regular basis.

Many people talk about this recent phenomenon in terms of an increase in evangelical "power," as if the goal of evangelical Christians is just to accumulate political capital and throw our weight around. Perhaps that is true for a few, but I think it misses our purpose entirely. We are not after personal power or fame. We do not have a personal need for attention, and we know that there is so much noise in the public debate of ideas that one more voice isn't vital. But we as Christians fundamentally appreciate freedom—not just for ourselves but for all people, in all places, all the time, and as we grow, we see that there are constant and powerful forces that are working to deny freedom to others. So it becomes our role to speak up. Why? Because we are the salt of the earth, the light of the world. We are carriers of the message of freedom, justice, goodness, and life. As ministers of reconciliation between God and humanity, we have a role that no one else can fill.

If the rise of evangelicalism continues, and Christian influence continues to increase, that's not just good news for evangelicals. It's good news for everyone.

, , , , ,

As I write, Pope John Paul II is being laid to rest in the grotto underneath St. Peter's Basilica in Rome. The media can speak of nothing else, and every major news Web site is updating with constant reports from Vatican City. The talk is of the pope's phenomenal gospel-oriented work in the last quarter-century. He wisely used his influence to help thwart Communism, defend the unborn, feed and clothe the poor, and embrace the world's youth. One of his early heralds to the world was, "Be not afraid!" He stood courageously against tyranny and encouraged Christians everywhere to adhere to traditional biblical principles. International journalists are recounting these issues right now, and as they do so, they have to contextualize the pope's significance for their audience. They explain what he represents to Catholics and how his life was dedicated to the public imitation of Jesus Christ.

The whole earth is contemplating the life of this man.

Now, it might seem odd to begin a book on contemporary evangelicalism with an observation about the pope, but we have entered a new day. I would not minimize the differences we Protestants have with the Catholic Church, but today those differences are not the point because the secular press is transfixed with the good works done by Pope John Paul II. The effect his life and death are having on the world and on people's perceptions of the gospel of Jesus Christ is pronounced. I love that this event is big news, because it means that observers the world over—even those who would prefer to ignore the importance of religion—are grappling with the effects of religious belief.

꙳꙳꙳꙳꙳

I believe that we are living in the midst of an unprecedented opportunity. We have a chance to pursue our primary purpose with newfound resolve.

꙳꙳꙳꙳꙳

This, as you likely know, is the trend in world events. Though for decades many scholars and journalists believed we were entering a new era of secularism, it is now clear that people all over the world still take faith seriously. Evangelicalism's rising influence and the attention given to the pope's death are just two aspects of a trend that shows no signs of waning. Most major events since the turn of the century have been embedded in religion—presidential elections, wars, the democratic Orange Revolution in Ukraine, and more.

Obviously religion is not always good news. Not nearly. Religion alone is not sufficient to spread liberty, promote justice, and enhance goodwill. But for those of us who have committed our lives to the completion of the Great Commission of Jesus, the fact that religion is in the air is good news, because it means that the gospel is never far from the conversation. It means we have abundant opportunity—more so than I have seen in my lifetime—to make statements of faith to ever-wider groups of people. It means we have a chance to represent the gospel on the world stage.

Several years ago, I wrote a book titled *Primary Purpose: Making It Hard for People to Go to Hell From Your City*. This book, along with three others (*Loving Your City into the Kingdom* by myself and Jack Hayford, *Taking Our Cities for God* by John Dawson, and *That None Shall Perish* by Ed Silvoso), was used to encourage the City-Strategy Movement of the 1990s.[1] Now, a decade later, evangelicalism is impacting society in an increasingly public and substantive way, not just within individual cities, but within entire nations.

This book is a revised and updated edition of *Primary Purpose*. The basic principles outlined in the first edition still apply, and much of that original material will be left untouched. I have updated stories and broadened the horizons in some places to reflect current global concerns, but our primary purpose is now what it always has been. Still, things have changed in the last decade. I believe that we are living in the midst of an unprecedented opportunity. Again, we cannot take the current level of interest in religion lightly. The events occurring around us constitute a chance to pursue our primary purpose with newfound resolve.

What is our primary purpose? I believe it is to do everything within our power to ensure that every person alive today has an opportunity to respond to the gospel. Ours is the first generation since Jesus gave the Great Commission that has the ability to communicate the gospel to every person on the planet. This is our generation's reason for being.

A couple of years ago, the *Atlantic Monthly* ran a cover story detailing the rise of conservative Christianity in the Southern Hemisphere. Philip Jenkins argued that Christianity will largely define world events throughout the next hundred years. "Christianity as a whole is growing and mutating in ways that observers in the West tend not to see," Jenkins wrote. "For obvious reasons, news reports today are filled with material about the influence of a resurgent and sometimes angry Islam. But it is Christianity, in its variety and vitality, in its global reach, in its association with the world's fastest-growing societies, in its shifting centers of gravity, in the way its values and practices vary from place to place—in these and other ways that will leave the deepest mark on the twenty-first century."[2]

Regardless of how *Atlantic* readers might feel about this, you and I know that this growth is the fruit of Christian missions and ministry in recent decades. The numbers do not indicate precisely what the quality of growth is like—that is, it is hard to measure the actual strength of all these local churches and new believers—but without a doubt, God is working in the hearts of men and women all over the world, and His kingdom is advancing.

Take a moment and think about what this means. You and I are alive during the most significant spread of Christianity in history. God is doing something wonderful in the earth, and we are part of it. How should we live our lives in response?

LIVING LIFE ACCORDING TO OUR PRIMARY PURPOSE

There are three questions we must ask ourselves if we are to live our lives according to our primary purpose. These three questions are fundamental to our direction in life—they shape our worldview and provide a foundation for all the work that we do.

1. *Where are we in time?* There is a timeline from the beginning of the world through all of human history until now. Different times call for different actions and perspectives. Too many people get stuck in the past or addicted to thinking about the future. We need to understand the moment we are living in and act accordingly. Great leaders throughout history understood the importance of this question and answered it correctly. Moses, Jesus, and Paul knew what they

needed to accomplish in their lifetimes. In the United States, George Washington, Abraham Lincoln, Dr. Martin Luther King Jr., Ronald Reagan, and others changed the world because they accurately understood what needed to happen in their day. We need to know the most important features, issues, and concerns of our era and work for the kingdom with those realities in view.

2. *What is God doing in our generation?* Where is He moving? What is He saying? Where is the hand of God at work? Think of the great work Christians have done in the last sixty or seventy years—the establishment of the National Association of Evangelicals; the rise of Billy Graham, Oral Roberts, Bill Bright, and many others; the Jesus Movement; the founding and strengthening of Christian colleges and universities; and more. We need to be a part of the very best work that God is doing in our generation. Think also of God's hand in global or political events—the sacrifices people made to win World War II and work for victory in the Cold War, for example, have produced a world with expanding representative governments, free-market wealth, and the spread of civil liberties. All this happens in God's timing, and it behooves us to be aware of what He is doing in the earth.

3. *What is our role in what God is doing?* This is where our thinking becomes actionable. What are we supposed to do with our lives? Where do we, as individuals, local churches, ministries, business owners, parents, students, and members of our community fit into God's plan for this generation? If we know where we are in time and accurately know what God is doing in our generation, then we have context for our lives. We can know how to act with specificity and intentionality. We know what to do with money, influence, time, relationships, and organizations. We will not waste our lives in wondering what we are supposed to do; we will know, and our lives will have purpose.

Those are "the big three," and as you can see, answering them gives shape, direction, and meaning to our lives. In the following chapters,

those questions will be in the background as you learn how to participate in all of our primary purpose. But before we move on to those
important principles, let me offer some specific thoughts on where we
are in time, what God is doing, and what we are called to do.

Of all generations in the history of the human race, ours may be
second only to the first century A.D. in terms of potential for the spread
of the gospel. The generation Jesus and His disciples lived in obviously
changed the world forever, but have you ever considered the political
and social realities that made that possible?

1. There was one superpower in the civilized world at the
   time—Rome.

2. Because there was one superpower, there was an extensive
   network of roads that provided opportunity for trade, which
   opened the door for the spread of the gospel. (The gospel
   often travels along routes of trade.)

3. Because there was one superpower, widespread communication was relatively easy.

Primarily because of these three facts, in the 150 years after the
ascension of Christ, the message of the gospel spread so dramatically
that Christianity was poised to become a global faith.

Now, let's look at our generation:

1. There is one superpower—the United States of America.

2. Because of this one superpower, pathways for global trade
   are opening. Again, trade opens doors for the gospel. When
   trade expanded to China, the church in China grew. When
   the Iron Curtain fell, the door was opened for trade, representative government, and freedom of religion; evangelicalism has since expanded throughout Eastern Europe.

3. Because of new technologies and the expansion of trade,
   global communication is easier than ever before. As a result,
   the gospel can be communicated more easily.

These are the major issues of our generation. It is absolutely crucial to recognize and embrace these realities, because Christians often get confused about where we are in time. The massive success of the novels in the Left Behind series is an indication of just how much people are captivated by any discussion of our place in history and how close we are to "the end." In fact, I fear that our generation is distracted by constant predictions and the endless search for last things and that such distractions keep us from doing the work on the ground. The fact is, we are still here. And we have unprecedented opportunity provided to us by the sovereignty of God. Eschatological escapism will not accomplish God's goals in the earth. Accurately discerning the times and fulfilling His plan for our generation will.

, , , , ,

What is our primary purpose? I believe it is to do everything within our power to insure that every person alive today has an opportunity to respond to the gospel.

, , , , ,

Remember when Jesus talked to the religious people of His day about this? He told them, "When you see a cloud rising in the west, immediately you say, 'It's going to rain,' and it does. And when the south wind blows, you say, 'It's going to be hot,' and it is. Hypocrites! You know how to interpret the appearance of the earth and the sky. How is it that you don't know how to interpret this present time?" (Luke 12:54–56). Jesus was telling them that they did not know that they were living at the most pivotal moment in human history. They had the Savior of the world among them, and they did not realize it.

You and I cannot let that happen to us. We need to know what God is doing around us and why. We must not be distracted.

DISCERNING THE TIMES

Scripture is fairly clear about how we will know the end is near. Matthew 24:14 says, "And this gospel of the kingdom will be preached in the whole world as a testimony to all nations, and then the end will come." I cannot say when the Lord will return, but I do believe we are living at the cusp of this verse. We are alive in a generation that is monumentally crucial to God's plan of salvation for humankind. We are developing the tools to communicate the gospel to every person on the earth. We could actually see the completion of the Great Commission.

Think about the markers of our generation:

1. We are experiencing the most massive growth of the church in history.

2. We are enjoying the greatest unity among Christians in over four hundred years.

3. We have greater resources available to the church than ever before.

4. More people live in nations that have constitutional protections for freedom of religion than ever before.

5. We have greater ease of travel worldwide than any previous generation.

6. We can communicate worldwide with greater ease and efficiency than in any previous generation.

7. We are coordinating unprecedented global prayer efforts.

Consider all this, and use it to frame the era in which you are living. Discern your times. The dominant world trends right now are opening the door for the fulfillment of the Great Commission. This is not the time for us to cower. This is the time to read our Bibles. This is the time to build churches. This is the time to pray. This is the time to press forward and advance the kingdom of God. This is our hour. With the rising influence of evangelicals around the world, the spread of Christianity throughout the Southern Hemisphere, and the increased pursuit of democracy and religious freedom throughout the world, God is working in our time, and we need to be a part of that work.

, , , , ,

We are alive in a generation that is monumentally crucial to God's plan of salvation for humankind.

, , , , ,

No doubt, there are negative developments as well. I don't deny the darkness that exists in the world. No question, there is a great deal of work to do. But God is working. Recently in *Christianity Today*, columnist Andy Crouch told a story of a ministry that is serving people in extraordinary ways. He wrote about a teenage girl named Elizabeth in Southeast Asia. Like too many young girls in that part of the world, Elizabeth was tricked into leaving her village by the promise of a well-paying job, and she ended up being forced into prostitution. For seven months, Elizabeth was trapped in a brothel and repeatedly raped.

But a Christian ministry called International Justice Mission focused their efforts on Elizabeth's situation, and they persuaded police to raid the brothel. Andy writes:

> When they arrived, they found that Elizabeth had written on the wall in her own language: "Ps. 27:1. The Lord is my light and my salvation. Whom shall I fear? The Lord is the strength of my life. Of whom shall I be afraid?" There were dozens more Scripture verses on the wall of Elizabeth's room—or, more accurately, her cell—all written by hand, taken from the Bible she read when not being forced to serve customers. But Psalm 27—describing the psalmist's trust in God even though "evildoers assail me to devour my flesh"—was what Elizabeth's rescuers saw and remembered.[3]

The story of Elizabeth is but one of thousands of stories that could be told about the work that Christians are doing throughout the earth. World Relief, the humanitarian arm of the National Association of Evangelicals, is often at the forefront of relief efforts wherever natural disasters or massive human rights violations occur. Similar organizations are working in virtually every corner of the earth, planting churches, building schools, and feeding the impoverished. Christians are also working strategically in places of political and cultural influence, including centers of art and entertainment from New York to Hollywood to Paris, leading academic institutions in the United States and abroad, and so on.

Encouraged yet? Clearly, I am no doomsayer. But neither do I have my head in the clouds. We have a lot of work ahead of us. People walk away from God every day. People make poor decisions and give their lives over to sin. The fact that evangelicals are being discussed does not mean that we are liked—in fact, it often means just the opposite. The fact that churches are being planted throughout the world does not always mean that those churches will survive or that they will be healthy, life-giving churches. We face threats from the rise of Islam, the popularity of religions such as Mormonism, the distracting power of consumer culture, and more.

But the Spirit of the Lord is moving. There is work to be done, and now is the time to do it. This is our primary purpose.

Two

How Love Makes
Everything Work

A FEW YEARS AGO, I was the guest speaker at the weeklong retreat for a fellowship of churches in Texas. This coalition of churches was filled with great pastors doing good work in small suburbs, exurbs, or rural communities. The biggest churches represented there held congregations of about 250 people, and the pastors were just as concerned with retaining their existing bodies of believers as they were with trying to add new people.

For most of the week, I taught each evening on some topic that would assist the pastors as they served their churches. I explained our free-market small group system at New Life. I explained how great children's and youth departments strengthen an entire church body. I explained how our church government structure serves the church and promotes creative change. I explained the crucial importance of having intercessors who are dedicated to praying for the church's pastors and staff members.

Every night the pastors asked fantastic questions after I spoke. We stayed up until the wee hours discussing how to improve their churches, and we continued our discussions over breakfast each morning. It was an informative, exciting retreat, and as the week wore on, I felt the pastors were ready to go home and really help the people in their churches. I thought they had what they needed to cause their congregations to grow.

But on the morning before the last service of the week, the president of the fellowship of churches pulled me aside. "Pastor Ted," he said, "the guys all feel like they have a lot to take away from this week. These principles are going to help all their ministries, and I'm excited for the future of our fellowship. Still, I can't help but thinking there's still something big that we're missing."

I told him I would be happy to devote the last session to anything he wanted me to discuss.

"That's great," he said. "I know this is going to sound simple, but what these guys really need to know about is love."

"What do you mean?" I asked.

"Our churches aren't growing much, and no doubt the systems and concepts you've explained this week will help. But I'm afraid none of it will really work unless our churches learn how to love. We have internal squabbles all the time. People are always taking sides against other people. We have a gossip problem throughout our fellowship. When someone makes a mistake, everyone knows about it. People are gracious with one another in person because that's part of the culture of the South, but behind closed doors we seem to delight in each other's problems.

"We are not living in love, and it's tearing us apart. It's making us ineffective and unable to serve the kingdom of God."

I knew exactly what he was talking about, and I knew he was right. Without love, nothing else would make sense. Without love, there was no hope of a healthy church government structure; there could not be a productive relationship between the senior pastor and youth pastor, or a truly powerful prayer ministry. Without a foundation of deep, real, and transformational love, church simply cannot work.

That night was the best night of the retreat. All the other principles and plans became actionable as we discussed the culture of love that every church needs. I told them how love is the engine that should drive hiring decisions, departmental shifts, ministry projects, budget priorities, and everything else that constitutes local church ministry. As this essential idea sank into the hearts and minds of the pastors in that room, I knew their churches would be reformed.

God is love. When we follow love, we are following God.

Even though there are wonderful discussions about the meaning and expression of love, I have simplified it. Love is living for someone else's good.

This book is filled with admonitions and advice that will work for you. You will gain focus for your primary purpose and insight into how to influence your community for Christ. I hope you will return to the principles in this book again and again.

, , , , ,

The degree to which you understand and live in love is the degree to which you will fulfill your primary purpose.

, , , , ,

But none of it will work the way it could if you do not grasp love. Nothing in these pages will be as effective as it could be if you make love the foundation of your life.

Love is not a sentimental emotion. It is an action, sometimes accompanied with warm feelings; other times it's just a decision that leads to an action. Love is always observable. It is doing something for the benefit of someone else. It's practical, it's observable, it's measurable. Love changes hearts, families, churches, businesses, and whole communities. So does the absence of love. The degree to which you understand and live in love is the degree to which you will fulfill your primary purpose.

I grew up in a rural Indiana community where love was an action. There was a culture of love that framed the entire town. Trust, respect, and admiration were central characteristics of our community. We took care of each other. We made sure everyone had enough food to eat and warm clothes to wear. Storeowners and homeowners alike left their doors unlocked. You could walk into a store after hours, pick up some items, and leave a note with some cash. It worked because no one was a threat to anyone else. We didn't gush with emotion, but we exemplified Christian love in our actions every day.

This is not just a warm memory of my childhood. I've taken the manifestation of love I remember in my hometown and implemented it into the ministry of New Life Church. We *do* tend to gush with emotion, but more than that, we live for each other's good—day in and day out. That's what it means to love.

THE DIVINE FLOW

Many years ago, I read a little booklet by John Osteen called *The Divine Flow*. As you likely know, John was a wonderful pastor who founded Lakewood Church in Houston, Texas, which is now the largest church in the nation and is led by John's son, Joel. John was a wonderful man who was ordained as a Southern Baptist and baptized in the Holy Spirit. In addition to serving as pastor at Lakewood, John hosted a weekly television program and wrote dozens of books and booklets.

The Divine Flow is only thirty-two pages long and probably took me twenty minutes to read, but it introduced a core idea that has shaped my life. John reminds us that often when Jesus ministered to people, the Scriptures indicate that He was moved with compassion (Matt. 9:36; 14:14; Mark 1:41; 6:34; 8:2; Luke 15:20). John explains that in those moments, Jesus was following a divine compulsion within Himself that drew Him to particular people. He did not go to people randomly. He was following the flow of divine love.

I think this "divine flow" is a key element of Christian ministry. If we follow the compulsion of love God places in us for other people, we will discover incredible friendships that will not only change our lives but also influence countless other lives. Why? Because the divine flow is not a random emotion. It is a strategic initiative God uses in us in order to accomplish certain tasks. He gives us love for people in order to join us together, and as we come together, we can get important work done for the kingdom.

At New Life Church, the divine flow is the principal characteristic of our staff and congregation. We flow in divine love for one another, and that love dictates the way we talk to each other, the way we spend time together, the projects we do, the culture of weekend services, and more. Our small groups are filled with the divine flow, as is each department. Love frames and drives everything we do.

Our church staff loves to eat together and laugh together. We are professionals, but professionalism never gets in the way of friendships, and neither do our friendships get in the way of work. We get lots of great work done *because* we love working together. Our love for each other is so genuine and deep that we function more like a family than a professional organization. We work efficiently, but we work so well together because our relationships are rooted in love. The kinds of problems that creep up in every organization creep up at New Life, too, but they are diffused quickly because we work in an atmosphere of love.

I seldom have to crack the whip or use any external motivation to get my staff to work. Actually, it's more common for me to have to crack the whip to make them *stop* working and go home to rest. They love being together so much that sometimes it's hard to get them to take a break.

The divine flow among our staff allows us to wear multiple hats with each other. From time to time over the years, Ross Parsley, our senior associate and worship pastor, has walked into my office and confronted me when I'm having a particularly, *um,* unsettling day—which means I've driven over a couple people and am too focused on a task to notice who is being left in my wake.

"Pastor Ted," he has said, smiling and leaning over my desk and looking me straight in the eye, "I'm taking off my associate pastor hat and putting on my friend hat. I'm here to tell you that you need to go home. It will be best for everyone if you don't talk to anyone else today. It will be best for the future of New Life Church if you go home, sit in a comfortable chair, and get yourself together. We love you, and we want to keep loving you, so go home and come back tomorrow."

Now, Ross could not say those things if he didn't love me and didn't know that I love him. And I couldn't respond in the right way—which is to nod silently, pack up my things, and head home—if I didn't love and trust him. Ross is one of my closest friends, and he's also my associate pastor. That delicate balance between friend and associate works because of the divine flow.

In all of this, the divine flow is being modeled for our congregation. New Life Church is rooted in deep love, appreciation, and respect. We are doing life together. We are a big family. We have good days together and bad days together. We go through wonderful times and difficult times. It all works because of real, genuine love.

OUR CALLING CARD

In His last discussion with His disciples, Jesus shared several big ideas that gave shape to the New Testament church. In John 13:4–8, we read about Jesus' shocking demonstration of love on the eve of the Passover:

> He got up from the meal, took off his outer clothing, and wrapped a towel around his waist. After that, he poured water into a basin and began to wash his disciples' feet, drying them with the towel that was wrapped around him.
>
> He came to Simon Peter, who said to him, "Lord, are you going to wash my feet?"
>
> Jesus replied, "You do not realize now what I am doing, but later you will understand."
>
> "No," said Peter, "you shall never wash my feet."
>
> Jesus answered, "Unless I wash you, you have no part with me."

Never the one to withhold comment, Peter's protestation surely captured everyone's hesitation. You can imagine the disciples shifting uneasily in their seats, thinking, *Jesus is the Messiah. We should be washing His feet. This isn't right at all!*

But Jesus was displaying the conditions for being part of His family of faith: the greatest becomes least, the leader serves the followers. When His disciples sought recognition, Jesus reminded them, "Whoever wants to be first must be slave of all. For even the Son of Man did not come to be served, but to serve, and to give his life as a ransom for many" (Mark 10:44–45).

He summarized this idea by exhorting His disciples to follow in His footsteps: "Love one another. As I have loved you, so you must love one another. By this all men will know that you are my disciples, if you love one another" (John 13:34–35). From this simple, familiar passage we get a profound idea. Christ's intent for the institution that would bear His name is that we would be known primarily not for our teaching or miracles or influence on civil government. The church's hallmark—our calling card—is the way we love one another.

It's tempting to leave it there. Love each other. But Jesus has more in mind. As it stands, there is nothing new about that commandment. His exhortation, if you look closer, is not merely that we love each other, but that we do it *the way He did it*. Not all love is the same—there are a number of varieties—and we should choose His.

Modern civilizations have organized themselves around watered down conventions of love. There are as many ways to "love" as there are to order a Starbucks coffee. We love handheld electronic devices, Lord of the Rings sequels, and overpriced half-sandwich combos at trendy fast-casual restaurants. We still love our spouses, children, and friends, but we also "love" stuff. Western civilization has propounded love, franchised it, merchandized it, and, ultimately, homogenized it. We are such a love-saturated society that the word means everything and nothing.

, , , , ,

Christ's intent for the institution that would bear His name is that we would be known primarily not for our teaching or miracles or influence on civil government. The church's hallmark—our calling card—is the way we love one another.

, , , , ,

Jesus anticipated this diluting of the idea of love. He commanded that the church's calling card not be merely to love one another, but to love one another the way He loved. He gave absolute definition to the word.

Incidentally, this is the same issue we're dealing with in America over the sacrament of marriage. In a society where some people want marriage to mean anything and everything, the church is faced with the task of defining the word *marriage* according to the institution it describes. Regardless of how others would like to define it, as Christians, our argument is that marriage means something particular: one man and one woman committed for a lifetime. In the same way that we have a specific, biblical definition of the word *marriage*, we have a specific, biblical definition of the word *love*. Jesus instructed us to be vanguards of His brand of love. He said, in essence, "Show the world My character by subordinating your own interests and living for other people's good. Define what love is according to My definition, and be walking, living examples of that love."

LIVING FOR SOMEONE ELSE'S GOOD

Jesus taught and modeled a brand of love that is both supernatural and ordinary. The perfect love of the Father flows into us through Jesus and manifests itself in average, mundane ways. Later in his life, John develops these ideas in his letters. His first epistle comments extensively on this incredible love that works in the heart of every believer. He says in 1 John 3:11–16:

> This is the message you heard from the beginning: We should love one another. Do not be like Cain, who belonged to the evil one and murdered his brother. And why did he murder him? Because his own actions were evil and his brother's were righteous. Do not be surprised, my brothers, if the world hates you. We know that we have passed from death to life, because we love our brothers. Anyone who does not love remains in death. Anyone who hates his brother is a murderer, and you know that no murderer has eternal life in him. This is how we know what love is: Jesus Christ laid down his life for us. And we ought to lay down our lives for our brothers.

As I said, an easy definition of love is to live for someone else's good. In John 3:16, the Bible tells us, "For God so loved the world that he gave his one and only Son, that whoever believes in him shall not perish but have eternal life." Here we see the love of God in action. God is giving His Son to take care of a problem that we can't rectify. He is doing something for our benefit, something that may or may not be to His own satisfaction, which is the evidence that He authentically loves us.

A few months ago, our staff discovered that some of our church's sound equipment was missing. A bit of investigation revealed that one of the young men in our congregation had been stealing our stuff—tens of thousands of dollars worth—so he and his buddies could start a band.

After discussing what to do with our team, I set up a meeting with the young man. He came into my office (nervously, of course), and as we talked, I felt a hint of God's affection for this boy. I felt a divine flow toward him. So I gave him a choice. He could either go to jail, or he could spend three days in the mountains praying and fasting with me. After getting over his surprise, he chose the fast.

We spent the time in the mountains praying, talking, and laughing. Actually, I was doing most of talking and laughing for the first day or so, but as he figured out that I really was *for* him, *for* his improvement, and *for* his future, he relaxed and was able to laugh with me. Eventually, the church got all the missing equipment back, and we were glad for it. But the real joy of this experience was the response of the boy and his family. They were relatively new to our church, but since this experience they have all connected deeply with our body. The young man is serving the Lord, and he and his parents are exceedingly grateful.

Now, I wasn't sitting around looking for something to do with my spare time on the day I heard about this kid. It would have been much more expedient—and perfectly sensible—to prosecute and let the law handle him. But to love is to live for another person's good. It didn't matter what was best for me. That young man was in a place in life where he could have gone either way. If he had gotten away with his crime, it would have been all too easy to continue down the road of perdition. If he had been caught and dealt with to the fullest extent of the law, his heart might have hardened against the church. As it is, he loves God, loves the church, and loves me! Love gave him a chance to respond to discipline wisely, and it changed him. He will tell this story for the rest of his life—the story of how love rescued him and showed him how to live for others.

QUALITY AND QUANTITY

Let's return to John's epistle. Later in the passage I referenced above, John continues his exhortation and explains that godly love expresses itself through action:

> If anyone has material possessions and sees his brother in need but has no pity on him, how can the love of God be in him? Dear children, let us not love with words or tongue but with actions and in truth.
>
> —1 JOHN 3:17–18

Love is an action, and it is a decision. It is intentional. We choose love as we choose our attitudes, careers, and outfits. In the same way we can be in the shower and think about what we are going to wear to work, we can also think about how we are going to love. We can premeditate it; it is observable; it is verifiable. Love is not just a feeling, which is why Jesus said in John 14:15, "If you love me, you will obey what I command." Jesus wants to see our love, just as we can see His. In Romans 5:8, the Bible says, "But God demonstrates his own love for us in this: While we were still sinners, Christ died for us."

Love is something we can qualify and quantify. There's no mystery to promoting or providing love. It's not invisible. We see it and hear it—or we recognize its absence—every day of our lives. Do people want to be around us? Do people know they can call on us? Are our friends, co-workers, and family members glad to see us when we walk into a room? Are we dependable? If we are living in love and accumulating a quantity of loving actions through the course of our daily lives, the answer to these questions is a resounding yes.

Quantity has a quality all its own. Love is something we build through intentional, specific acts. A popular bumper sticker of our day says, "Practice random acts of kindness." That idea is the opposite of intentional love. What we are after is a steady stream of acts of love that others can see. Love is predictable and reliable. Love is regular—it's something we do again and again and again. Over time, a great quantity of loving acts builds into a quality that is deep and sure.

Grasp this idea. Embrace it and practice it, and it will be the engine that drives everything else in your life.

THREE

THE LOCAL CHURCH
NEEDS YOU!

JESUS CHANGED MY life. I was raised in a liberal church that did not emphasize the importance of being born again. Then, when I heard about a personal relationship with Christ and the centrality of the Bible, my life began to transform. I believe what the Bible says about renewing our minds; therefore, I've embarked on a lifelong study of God's Word in order to know the way God thinks. I believe what the Bible says about transformation of the inner man; therefore, I enjoy prayer time each morning where the life of God can flow into my life. I am different because of Jesus. I am the living proof that Jesus is alive. He has transformed me. He is everything good that is in me.

But God knows that my personal relationship with Him is not all there is to Christian living. I do not function independently of others. Even though I have a wonderful, unique relationship with God, and even though I read my Bible, have a private prayer life, and am responsible for my own integrity, I am just one member of a larger family. I am part of the body of Christ, and I am connected to a local family of believers. And as a member of that family, I'm part of a series of relationships that causes the gospel to spread to everyone within our collective reach.

The subject of this book is our primary purpose, and we have discussed how the goal of our generation is to do all we can to fulfill the Great Commission. As we communicate the gospel, it transforms people's lives just as it has transformed your life and my life. When the gospel touches enough of the lives around us, then our community begins to change.

For this reason, the local church is the best tool for social change. Churches are charged with spreading the gospel to their communities, not just through evangelistic outreach, but through consistent, life-giving witness to the love of God. Over the days, weeks, months, years, and decades of a church's existence, it should become the core of its community. As churches do their jobs well, crime rates should fall, businesses should flourish, poverty should decline, education should improve, families should strengthen, and people should generally live better, more successful lives.

I address this here because within Christian culture today there is some confusion about the various roles of organizations within the body. Even though everyone is doing great work, unnecessary tension creeps up between local churches and parachurch ministries like Focus on the Family or Campus Crusade for Christ. It is unfortunate, because parachurch ministries (which I prefer to call "servant church ministries" or "mission church ministries") serve clear and important functions. Bill Bright led me to the Lord when I was a sixteen-year-old attendee of Explo '72 in Dallas, Texas. He ministered to me not as a local church pastor but as an executive leader of Campus Crusade. Billy Graham reached my dad for Christ as a mission church evangelist, not a local pastor. Many people are born again, and many more receive material or spiritual assistance because of the work of parachurch organizations.

Still, they are not the local church. They *are* part of the overall, united church of God, but in organizational and missional terms, they do not perform the same task as the local church and should be considered different.

TIMES HAVE CHANGED

Let me review some history for you. In the 1960s, mainline churches dominated virtually every American city. These churches were organized by the National Council of Churches (NCC), and over time, they became increasingly liberal. Even though many of them had been evangelical in their earlier years, these churches stopped teaching the integrity of the Bible, the authority of Christ, or the necessity of being born again. As a result, God moved in the hearts of several Bible-believing men and women to develop parachurch ministries to emphasize the integrity of God's Word, a high view of Christ, and the necessity of being born again; they promoted evangelicalism in America. While this was going on, a great movement was underway to establish solid evangelical churches and the necessary infrastructure (schools, media outlets, publishing houses, and so on) to support evangelicalism. Most of these churches and groups were related to the conservative organization the National Association of Evangelicals. In time, the mainline denominations experienced a major decline. Today, the largest churches in nearly every American city are evangelical.

SO, WHAT IS A PARACHURCH MINISTRY?

Parachurch organizations, then, are not mere side projects, and they are not isolated ministries. In the last half-century, God has used parachurch ministries to bolster and maintain life-giving local churches. As mission organizations and servant ministries have experienced massive growth and developed identities of their own, local churches have been strengthened and, in several cases, have morphed into megachurches. Thus, local churches and parachurch ministries enjoy a symbiotic relationship—they mutually benefit one another and work together for the common good of the kingdom.

So what's the problem? Well, there is a conflict here, and as with many issues, it partly comes down to money. Many American evangelicals are conflicted about whom they should financially support—parachurch ministry organizations or their local church. I think each believer's responsibility is clear: tithe 10 percent to the local church, and give additional offerings to parachurch ministries. The local church is the storehouse, the backbone, and the foundation for all ministry, which means that local churches should also financially contribute to the parachurch ministries that are consistent with their mission. So parachurch funding should come from two sources: offerings from God's people and local churches. Local churches, on the other hand, should be the recipients of 100 percent of the tithe. As long as we recognize how the local church differs from parachurch organizations, there should never be any confusion for how to support each. Here are a few ways to tell the difference between them.

The local church is a family. Parachurch ministries are a project.

In the local church we have old people, young people, smart people, dull people, happy people, sad people, competent people, irresponsible people, great people, and average people. It's a family. It can be messy. But it is there for the long haul, through all of life's stages and the whole variety of issues we face from birth to death.

Parachurch ministries are different. Parachurch ministries focus on one or maybe a few specific projects that sharpen their purpose and role. They have the delight of having a specific purpose that they have to fulfill. Focus on the Family deals with issues that impact the family. Compassion International feeds and cares for children in Jesus' name. Young Life builds Christian campus clubs in schools across America. Campus Crusade reaches out to college kids. Wycliffe translates the Bible. World Relief provides Christian relief and development. On and on it goes. All of these ministries do more than I've described here, but the idea is clear: *they do specific projects*. Everything they do is intended to strengthen and undergird the local church. No doubt, they support the ministry of the local church, but they are not local churches.

The local church is like a light bulb. Parachurch ministries are like a laser.

Local church ministry provides general light to everyone in their various stages of life and their various situations. It is general light, and it's useful for an endless number of projects. Parachurch ministry is also light, but it's more focused. Parachurch ministries are often easier to define and observe. They can state their role in a sentence or two. A local church is broader and more general. Typically, when a pastor or local church employee goes to work, that person doesn't have any idea what he or she will end up doing that day, because local church ministry does so many different and unpredictable things. It is there to serve and strengthen the diversity of the whole family. In contrast, a parachurch ministry employee has a much clearer picture of his or her assignment. The parachurch ministry provides expertise to the local church, but it is not the local church.

⟩⟩⟩⟩⟩

The local church is one of the greatest tools a God gives us to fulfill our primary purpose.

⟩⟩⟩⟩⟩

A local church is like a general practitioner. A parachurch ministry is like a medical specialist.

A good general practitioner is the place to start and end with our medical needs. Anything from a cold to the flu to a broken bone can be taken care of by the family doctor. But when something arises that needs particular care, our family practitioner refers us to a specialist. If we need eyeglasses, we go to an ophthalmologist. If we have a difficult skin condition, we go to a dermatologist. If we are having a baby, we need an obstetrician. This is the way a local church and a parachurch ministry should relate to one another. We need them both, but they perform different functions. The specialist can never replace the family doctor, and the family doctor needs the specialist to assist in particular situations.

Again, the only reason any of this is a problem is that people get confused about whether they should support parachurch ministries with their tithe dollars. But the local church suffers when parachurch ministries creep into tithing funds. In the United States, we have more evangelical parachurch ministries than anywhere else in the world, but we are not seeing the church growth that we would like. Why? In part, it is because we all need to devote ourselves to healthy, life-giving local churches as well as parachurch ministries that are authentically moving us forward.

I have spoken with pastors of some of the world's largest megachurches—I call them *super-megachurches*. They tell me that sometimes when American parachurch ministries think they are doing good works for God's kingdom, they are in fact weakening the kingdom. They feel this is primarily because parachurch ministries focus on their specific goals without the context or understanding of healthy life relationships that should provide texture to their efforts. They are not local church people. As a result, in the midst of their good work, they unintentionally keep local evangelical churches from advancing as they should, thus keeping the kingdom from being able to advance in any one neighborhood in the name of a national or global project that is compelling to donors. They believe, as I do, that communities are transformed primarily through the ministry that occurs though healthy local churches, but that American Christians, because we have project-mindedness instead of family-mindedness, don't even know what an authentic local church family life is like.

In other words, we Christians are motivated to give partly by our level of excitement about one project or another. That is not necessarily a problem, but it becomes a problem if our excitement about an outreach to a single relief cause restricts our commitment to our local church. And unfortunately, this kind of problem has become endemic to parachurch fund-raising in America.

Look around, and you will see that it is true.

- Many evangelical foundations will not finance local church projects.

- Many major donors do not tithe to their local churches.

- Many ministers form parachurch ministries and divert attention away from their home church.

- Some of the brightest and most innovative young men and women envision themselves doing parachurch work rather than running strong local churches.

So where does this leave us? With our money and brightest young people investing in specialized ministry rather than developing and sustaining the core of family life.

What must we do? Understand that since the beginning of the

church, we have had both the parachurch and local church ministries working in harmony with one another, and that needs to continue in strength today. How? By tithing to the local church, no matter how much we earn, and supporting the helpful work of good parachurch ministries with our offerings (above and beyond our tithe) and with some of the funds in the storehouse.

What's the key here? Tithe 10 percent of our income to our local church and then, if we can, give to parachurch ministry. If we want to give to parachurch ministries, that giving should come from funds other than the tithe.

, , , , ,

We cannot forget to reach *someone* in the midst of reaching *everyone*.

, , , , ,

Local churches provide a place where believers become family—where they can practice their love for each other, be tested, and help each other grow to maturity in Christ. The local church is one of the greatest tools God gives us to fulfill our primary purpose.

Participate in your local church. Don't just attend. Be part of the family. Teach, connect, become involved. Ensure that in the midst of reaching the whole country or whole world, you also authentically reach one neighborhood. I have been exposed to national initiatives all my life that do widespread things but don't reach any concentrated area; as a result, these initiatives might not produce as much as we could have produced by emphasizing at least one neighborhood. We cannot forget to reach *someone* in the midst of reaching *everyone*.

This is the generation that can do it. This is the generation that can fulfill our purpose of spreading the gospel to everyone. We can do it, with love, if we will do it by building and sustaining life-giving local churches.

—Section II—

Making It Hard to Go to Hell From Your City

EARLY THREE YEARS ago I was elected president of the National Association of Evangelicals (NAE). The election was surprising to me because this sixty-year-old organization is comprised primarily of church denominations. It represents thirty million people who meet in forty-five thousand churches from more than fifty evangelical denominations. This group is made up of the Assemblies of God, the Evangelical Free Church of America, The Salvation Army, the International Pentecostal Holiness Church, the Christian and Missionary Alliance, the International Church of the Foursquare Gospel, the Presbyterian Church in America, The Wesleyan Church, Open Bible Churches, and many other fine groups. I am supportive of these groups, but, because of my background, I was surprised they chose me.

I am Southern Baptist, which is the largest evangelical group that is not a member of the NAE. I pastor an independent charismatic church, which, historically, has been a contrasting group from the classical Pentecostal groups that make up some of the core of the NAE. So, when the executive committee asked me to serve as president, I listed four significant reasons why, in my mind, I was a bad choice. They smiled, said that none of those reasons were meaningful to them, and asked me to serve. Then, six months later, the entire board of directors of the NAE had an opportunity to vote on my presidency, and, for the first time in over sixty years, 100 percent of the board affirmed someone in the role as president.

I have served with this group of leaders for a number of years as an NAE member, board member, executive committee member, and now as president. As I look at people like Bill Hammel from the Evangelical Free Church; Steve Machia from Vision New England and Leadership Transformations, Inc.; Leith Anderson from Wooddale Church in Minneapolis, Minnesota; Don Duff, a successful businessman who has supported the NAE for decades; David Holdron, general superintendent of The Wesleyan Church; Todd Bassett from The Salvation Army; Tom Trask from the Assemblies of God; and Roy Taylor from the Presbyterian Church in America, I see a broad range of theological and cultural streams. But they work together, enjoy each other, and see the importance of unified evangelical action. In order to work together, they and their groups have to stretch and overcome differences. They have done this well.

Last fall I went to Pattaya, Thailand, for the meeting of the Lausanne Committee for World Evangelization, a global evangelical strategy group. The room was full of Calvinists and Armenians, Pentecostals and cessationists—and they were all enjoying one another. As Vonette Bright led in prayer and Paul Ceder exhorted us to action, the unity and strength of the global church was apparent.

A few weeks later I flew to London to meet with Luis Bush and a team of leaders working to mobilize Christians from various roles in life to actually transform their nations, not just with spiritual renewal, but with the other exhortations from Scripture that make life better for people. These believers, who work with people from every imaginable stream in the body of Christ, spoke about the successes and opportunities presenting themselves around the globe and what it would take to coordinate a global transformation movement. Luis and the others were cooperating to ensure that the advance of the gospel transforms society in a way that will help all people.

These strategists were a diverse bunch, but they were united under a common cause.

As I observed these people and thought about other groups that are getting so much done for the cause of Christ, I realized something: the very principles that we stumbled upon years ago trying "to make it hard to go to hell from Colorado Springs" were the same principles that were being embraced by these global leaders.

The first of these principles is that we focus on the absolutes of the Scriptures. In other words, we stop highlighting our differences and capitalize on the biblical essentials common to all genuine evangelicals.

Second, we determine to promote Christ and His Word above our own particular church or way of doing things.

Third, we pray in order to raise "the water level of the Holy Spirit's work worldwide." In other words, we pray for more and more of God's work to be done so that people will be drawn into the kingdom of God. We measure the efficacy of our prayer in observable ways, such as increased church attendance.

Fourth, we appreciate one another's respected interpretations of Scripture. I call them "respected interpretations" because heresy is not tolerated, nor is theological liberalism. But "respected interpretations," which are interpretations supported by mainstream evangelical biblical scholarship, are fine—even welcomed. These leaders recognize that some true believers embrace various interpretations that others reject.

Fifth, we practice supportive speech and actions toward one another. This principle is fundamental to the success of every family, including the family of God.

When I go to meetings with the NAE, the Lausanne Committee, or the Transformations Movement, I see the same scene over and over again. Local church and parachurch leaders of all varieties are standing in small groups laughing and talking. They greet each other with hugs, handshakes, and smiles, and they welcome new people into their groups.

How can people with such diverse beliefs do this? They worship differently, attend different churches, and have totally different understandings of the Scriptures. But they are applying the same principles that the Lord was highlighting to church leaders in Colorado Springs over a decade ago. I've seen these five principles—which I am about to discuss even further with you in the next five chapters of this book— at work for years. They are simple. They are practical. And they are proven.

—Four—

Focus on the Absolutes of Scripture

(Principle #1)

Absolutes are the essential beliefs that are central to Christianity. We all agree that Jesus of Nazareth is the Messiah and that He came in the flesh to destroy the works of the devil (1 John 3:8). We know that through Him we have access to the Father and, therefore, eternal life (Eph. 2:18). In addition, we all believe the Bible is the primary source of information about God, and it is the standard we use to judge spiritual experiences and teaching (2 Tim. 3:16).

In other words, we believe Jesus Christ is the truth. He is the fact every human being must face. We also believe the Bible is the inspired Word of God.

Absolutes are the nonnegotiable core tenets of Christian faith. These ideas are the sword to fall on, the hill to die on. Absolutes are not subject to personal convictions, cultural trends, or even feelings. People commit their lives to Jesus today the same way they always have. They come to Him in humble submission, turn from the world, and confess His lordship. That's why the first principle that enables us to work together in the body of Christ is to focus on the absolutes of Scripture. When we focus on absolutes, we are in agreement.

One of the first tasks I faced as NAE president was to define for a newly interested news media just what an evangelical is. It seemed like an elementary question, but after pondering it and bouncing it off other leaders from Nazarene to Pentecostal, I came to realize that we needed to fine-tune our definition. What is an evangelical? What handful of core ideas unifies such a vast and varied constituency?

We reduced the definition to three simple truths that I mentioned earlier. An evangelical is a Christian believer who: (1) believes that Jesus Christ is the Son of God; (2) believes the Bible is the Word of God; and (3) believes in the necessity of being born again.

Now understand, this is not to say that there are not additional core beliefs. Yet these three ideas are the core, nonnegotiable, fall-on-your-sword tenets of evangelicalism. They are three of our absolutes.

Evangelical Christianity is broad enough to encompass Bob Jones, Benny Hinn, and the vast gamut of thought and expression in between, all built upon the same absolutes. By agreeing to focus on the absolutes of Scripture, all expressions of orthodox Christianity can work together with confidence that none of us is being required to forsake core beliefs.

Look at Illustration 1 on page 37. Everything we Christians believe fits somewhere in one of the four areas described.

, , , , ,

By agreeing to focus on the absolutes of Scripture, all expressions of orthodox Christianity can work together with confidence that none of us is being required to forsake core beliefs.

, , , , ,

At the center are the absolutes, the unchanging foundations of faith.

The next circle includes interpretations. An interpretation consists of an explanation and application of the Scripture. We usually are interpreting when we read a passage of Scripture and then say, "Now this is what it means." There are often several respected interpretations of a Scripture passage. An interpretation may be wrong, but an absolute is never wrong.

Illustration 1

DIAGRAM OF AN INDIVIDUAL'S BELIEF SYSTEM

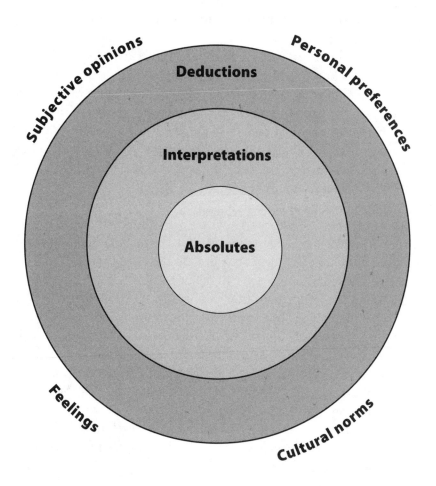

Then there are deductions. Deductions come from looking at several passages of Scripture and drawing conclusions. We look at one passage in the Bible and draw interpretation A; then we look at another passage somewhere else and draw interpretation B; and then we consider the two together and conclude that A + B = C. A deduction is a theological construction of two or more interpretations. Absolutes are more certain than interpretations. Interpretations are more certain than deductions.

Finally, there are subjective opinions, which are personal preferences, such as how long a church service should be or what styles of songs we should sing. Sometimes taking opinions too seriously gets ridiculous. For example, I know of a church in Mississippi that split over whether to put a hat rack in the lobby. During a business meeting at a church in Indiana, one church leader's wife slapped another leader's wife while they were debating over the need for gutters on the outside of the building.

The absolutes are our core, but interpretations, deductions, and subjective opinions divide us. Certainly we will have interpretations, deductions, and subjective opinions. But we make a grave mistake when we don't separate them according to their importance.

All biblical Christians believe in the importance of the Holy Spirit. Some prefer speaking about the "baptism in the Holy Spirit," while others promote being "filled with the Holy Spirit." Some like "being controlled by the Holy Spirit," while others discuss "fellowship with the Holy Spirit." All realize the absolute necessity of the Holy Spirit's ministry, but because of various interpretations, deductions, and subjective opinions about the scriptures that refer to the Holy Spirit, we have a differing emphasis on His ministry.

Believing the same absolutes, we differ on interpretation. That's why we have Christians who believe there is no biblical basis for the operation of such gifts as tongues or words of knowledge in this generation (cessationists). We also have Christians who believe all the gifts have the potential for full expression in the church today just as they did in the early church (Pentecostals and charismatics).

ABSOLUTES CONFUSED
WITH OTHER BELIEFS

I once heard a pastor teach about how Christians would be taken up in a rapture and enjoy the marriage supper of the Lamb for seven years while those left on Earth would go through horrible tribulation. Then, at the end of the seven years, Jesus and the raptured Christians would appear in the eastern sky, victoriously returning to begin the Millennium. What amazed me was how he ended his sermon. He said, "If it doesn't happen this way, then Jesus Christ is not Lord."

This brother was equating deductions with an absolute.

The events of Christ's return may happen just as those who embrace pretribulation rapture theology predict. But whether or not the events occur in that precise fashion, Jesus is still Lord.

Most of what is taught as End-Times theology is deductions.

The lordship of Jesus Christ is an absolute.

Deductions are interesting, sometimes even helpful to our understanding of Scripture, but they are not the same as absolutes; they are not as certain.

However, this brother wasn't making this distinction in his own mind, so those who were influenced by his teaching probably would not make the distinction in their own thinking either. And without this clarification being made, this pastor and his students may reasonably conclude that if some people don't believe in pretribulation eschatology, then they are not biblical Christians. That would be a horrible mistake, because they would become unable to identify the body of Christ in their own community and around the world. If we Christians can't even identify each other, it becomes very difficult to know if we are expanding God's kingdom effectively or not.

So we must not confuse what the Bible actually says with what we think it means, because our culture and our subjective opinions influence our thinking processes.

While in Moscow several years ago I met some Christians who believed that it was an ungodly, sinful act to wear a tie. They believed it so strongly that they didn't think any genuine Christian could ever wear a tie because it pointed toward hell. I thought that was ridiculous and purely cultural and was proud that we in the West were so much more rational...until I heard an American pastor talking about how significant his new church steeple was "because it pointed to heaven." His logic was identical to that of the brothers in Moscow! Both valued their purely cultural position.

, , , , ,

Our identity as Christians must be based consciously on the absolute core of our faith: Jesus Christ and the Word of God, the Bible.

, , , , ,

We are destroying our potential for impacting the spiritual climate by highlighting our differences on nonessential issues. They unnecessarily divide us. We preach so vigorously on interpretations, but we sometimes fail to understand that our greatest strength is in the absolutes. When we believers start comparing ourselves to others on the basis of interpretations rather than absolutes, our influence is weakened.

Even though our nonessentials do have importance, they must never become the source of our identity. Our identity as Christians must be based consciously on the absolute core of our faith: Jesus Christ and the Word of God, the Bible.

If anyone equates interpretations with absolutes, that person will soon have a crisis of faith when one of his interpretations is challenged or proven false.

Several years ago, I met with a young couple who had a friend who told them the only true Bible is the King James Version of the Bible. They were alarmed because our church uses the New International Version, which they had been told was not really a Bible at all.

I drew the three circles on a board for them, and we placed their items of concern in appropriate circles. When they saw that salvation issues were in the absolutes circle and their friend's opinions about the King James Version fell in the area of subjective opinions and cultural norms, they understood. Their fears were relieved. Obviously, their friend was making a horrible mistake by equating absolutes with a preference.

DO DOGS GO TO HEAVEN?

When I was in high school, my younger sister, Mary Lois, had a pet dog that died. I received the assignment of digging the grave and conducting a funeral service for the dog.

After a beautiful funeral, through her tears my cute little sister asked me if she would see her dog in heaven. I answered by explaining that dogs do not go to heaven because they don't have spirits and, therefore, cannot receive eternal life as we human beings do. So, I concluded for her, her dog was gone—dust—never to be seen again.

She broke into deep sobs and ran into the house. Subsequently, my dad threatened to give me the only spanking I would have received during my teen years. While contemplating potential pain, the revelation struck me that no one knew with absolute certainty whether or not dogs go to heaven. Certainly those questions don't have the same level of importance as, say, questions about Jesus' lordship and the integrity of God's Word, but they have relevance. I believe pastors can and should preach on more than the absolutes, but the congregations need to understand what they're doing.

When I'm teaching on an absolute, I say, "The Bible says…"

When transitioning into an interpretation, I say, "I believe this means…" or, "Many Bible scholars believe…"

If I am teaching a deduction, I usually say something like, "From these Scripture verses we conclude…"

As the congregation hears these distinctions, they realize the body of Christ includes all who believe the same absolutes, although individuals, churches, and movements may differ in interpretations or deductions.

But if people learn that the only true Christians are those who share their specific interpretations and deductions, then they must exclude from their Christian fellowship practically everyone. Not only would they avoid networking with other churches, but also they probably couldn't talk to most of the people in their own church!

We must all resist the temptation to teach or even imply that our deductions have equal importance with absolutes. Now, I realize that very few people teach material knowing it is untrue. But I don't know anyone who, reflecting on his own opinions of ten years earlier, would agree with everything he believed then, except, of course, for the absolutes.

SUBJECTIVE OPINIONS

What role do subjective opinions play? Unfortunately, most people use their feelings to choose their local church. That's acceptable only as long as the church is grounded in the absolutes. I suspect that even though some people may say that the Lord led them to one church or another, it is often a matter of their being comfortable in the cultural setting a particular church affords them. In some cases they have come to believe a certain setting is "where God is" because of their cultural expectations.

The church I pastor has its own culture. It feels somewhat like an international convention center. All types of people attend, from those who wear cut-off shorts, sandals, and tank tops to those who wear very expensive suits and dresses. Many economic, educational, and ethnic groups are represented in our congregation. There is no choir loft or stained glass. Some people feel comfortable at New Life Church, while others feel more comfortable in a traditional setting.

The church is—and should be—as diverse in its subjective opinions as the human race itself. Within the last couple of years, I spoke at one large church conference in Taipei, Taiwan, and another in Lagos, Nigeria. Over the course of the four-day conference in Taipei, I learned that the Taiwanese pastors' gesture of highest appreciation was sitting absolutely silent and motionless, spectacles on, Bible and notebook open in their lap, listening intently. The Nigerian pastors, by contrast, communicated that they were with you and receiving from the Lord by standing up and blowing whistles in deafening unison! Both groups loved Jesus. Both loved the Scriptures, the ministry of the local church, and the advance of the kingdom of God in their generation. Each expressed enthusiasm for the things of God according to their own system of subjective values.

Every one of us has a cultural norm that we use as a standard for our Christian worship and study. These cultural norms are not necessarily biblical or contrary to the Bible; they are simply cultural. They are neither good nor bad, as long as we don't equate our religious cultural norms with the essence of our faith.

Heaven is our home, and Earth is our mission. So we must be willing to understand and work within Earth's cultures. At the same time, we need to caution against conflating our own cultural heritage with the absolutes of the Scriptures. When we recognize this, it's easier to work with others who have different worship styles than we do, because we know our differences are less important than the absolutes.

OUR PRIMARY PURPOSE

Inside the walls of our churches, let's teach and practice the full menu of what we believe. Let's fully enjoy the security of the absolutes. Let's express and practice our interpretations and deductions. In addition, let's rejoice in our cultural and personal preferences in worship and teaching.

But outside the walls of our individual churches, I believe we must focus on the absolutes. When we do, we put tremendous pressure on the forces of evil that want to divide us and distract us from our primary purpose.

〉〉〉〉〉

**The absolutes of Scripture
are what the world needs.**

〉〉〉〉〉

The result is that the non-Christian community hears the same basic absolutes from thousands of Christians from a variety of churches. They start wondering where all the Christians have come from. No longer are they hearing that Baptists are better than Presbyterians or that charismatics are more spiritual than Lutherans. Instead, they hear from all of these groups that Jesus is the only solution to the problems they face and that they can trust the Bible.

During the 2004 presidential election, much of the news analysis pointed to the evangelical vote as the pivotal factor in the election's outcome. Suddenly, news media far and wide wanted to talk about Christianity in America. I knew that our greatest window of opportunity for presenting a united front was also our greatest moment of vulnerability to painting a picture of a fractured, ineffective church. One evening I was being interviewed on Fox News at the same time Rick Warren was just down the dial on CNN. Both of us were being questioned about the phenomenon of evangelicalism in America. Rick Warren, serving a Southern Baptist Church, and I, serving an independent charismatic church, could easily have defined ourselves by our distinctives. Thankfully, each of us focused instead on the absolutes of Christian belief and expression, and America received a clear, unified picture.

The absolutes of Scripture are what the world needs. Once people come to Christ and into our churches, then they can make choices about interpretations, deductions, and culture.

I believe Christians and non-Christians alike are fed up with judgmental remarks about other churches and Christians and what they believe. They get excited, instead, when they see church leaders and members of different churches working together to serve our common primary purpose.

—FIVE—

PROMOTE THE MINISTRY OF CHRIST AND HIS WORD ABOVE OUR OWN MISSION OR METHOD

(PRINCIPLE #2)

W E'VE ALL SEEN the church ads that tout, "Best choir," "Friendliest pastor" or "New sanctuary." Do we want to convince the world that our church or our style is better than all others? Or do we want to work in harmony with other life-giving churches to convince as many as possible that Jesus is alive?

People say, "Come to the men's meeting at our church; it's the best one in the city," or "Such and such church has the best youth pastor."

Why are we so comparative?

Sometimes we unknowingly encourage this type of comparative thinking. We communicate that our church teaches correct doctrine and has the most complete understanding on any given subject. But we don't realize the confusion we create. Most people are exposed to other fine Christians who radically differ from us on some interpretations, deductions, or subjective values. Even worse is the message that is communicated to non-Christians: "If Christians can't agree with other Christians, how can I trust that they are telling me the truth?"

A LUXURY WE CANNOT AFFORD

Never forget that the church is in a battle. All over the world Satan is using some strategy to make it hard for people to go to heaven. It may be secularism, Islamic fundamentalism, humanism, pornography, rampant crime, poverty, prosperity, apathy, self-righteousness, religion, or any other snare. With so much at stake and so much confusion in the air, the church has to be single-minded in its task of witnessing to the truth of the gospel.

Today, some self-appointed evangelical "watchdog" organizations spend all their energies enumerating the differences among evangelicals. They are professional faultfinders. No doubt, we need to monitor the integrity of the various messages within the body, but we also need to work together and encourage one another. We need each other. It's not like the days when God-consciousness was reinforced by prayer in schools, at athletic events, and during graduation ceremonies. Today, more than ever, we need a unified front.

In the pre-1960s' Judeo-Christian culture of America, the church forgot its primary purpose. The average American community only had Christian churches. Sometimes a small Jewish synagogue would be present, but there were no Islamic mosques or Hindu temples. The vast majority of people were Methodist, Baptist, Presbyterian, Mennonite, or members of some other mainline Christian group. Perhaps because we were comfortable, we believed that comparing ourselves against ourselves was a significant task, even more significant than doing the actual work of the gospel. But because the church was so consumed with itself, the Christian message lost influence.

Now America is different. Islam is the fastest-growing religion in several American cities. Hinduism and Buddhism are being taught in our schools and are patently embraced in some areas of our culture. In education, secular thought is respected; religious thought is scorned.

In some Christian circles today, believers don't accept the fact that America has changed. In fact, many times we actually use our churches to protect a culture that is long gone. Rather than rethinking our methods, challenging our own effectiveness, and expanding our vision to a global charge, we try to escape responsibility for the eternal damnation of those around the world by blaming others for our own spiritual ineffectiveness.

But we Christians no longer have the luxury of spending time talking so much about the differences between us. We are missing too many opportunities around the world. We have unprecedented opportunities in Afghanistan, Iraq, Lebanon, and elsewhere. We have open doors that were distant dreams a few years ago in Eastern Europe. If we keep missing these opportunities, our own communities will begin to suffer. Most haven't realized the danger of missed opportunity because our church buildings are still standing and we are so busy doing good things. But being busy has nothing to do with whether or not we have any impact on our world. It's time for all of us to make the main thing the main thing.

Several times every week I have to ask myself this: Is what I'm doing really something that will make a difference in someone else's eternal destiny? Does it pass the "who cares" test? Does it promote Christ and His Word in our community? Will it help the non-Christians in the community understand the message of Christ?

ʼ ʼ ʼ ʼ ʼ

Being busy has nothing to do with whether or not we have any impact on our world.

ʼ ʼ ʼ ʼ ʼ

It doesn't matter how great my program, church, or actions are in comparison to those of any other Christian. My mission is to communicate a timeless message in a changing culture.

THE CULTURAL WALL

Even though Christian radio and television are invaluable tools for the fulfillment of the Great Commission, most non-Christians aren't listening to Christian radio stations or watching Christian television programs. They don't understand Christian jargon, and they don't care about most Christian squabbles. There's a cultural wall between "us" and "them."

I believe we Christians often fail to communicate to non-Christians because we are broadcasting on a different channel, both literally and figuratively. Non-Christians do, however, know when they are hurting and need help.

Over the past year, we've run a few different secular radio and TV spots built around the theme "Come Home." We felt that in today's fast-paced world, it is easy to feel disconnected and alone. Amidst the frantic pace, it's sometimes hard to know where and how to rest. We wanted people to know that church is a place where they can come to find rest and a sense of belonging. One of the ads was specifically focused on helping people find help with everyday sorts of things—from finances to career guidance. We wanted people to know that church is much more than a Sunday morning service; it's an opportunity to form relationships that bring much-needed support and "coaching" into our lives. That's a message that is meaningful to an unsaved person. Everybody needs a little help with life.

, , , , ,

An ad on the religion page will help a few people who are looking for special events or would like to find a new church home, but it doesn't make much of a dent in our primary purpose.

, , , , ,

One Christmas season, one of our spots for secular radio encouraged people to give their families one of the greatest gifts a person could give—the gift of good character. The ad explained that by becoming a person who keeps his word, stays faithful to his spouse, and learns to care for the needs of others, we give the people who are in relationship with us a gift that lasts a lifetime. That was the whole point of the ad—there was no gospel presentation, no "come to New Life Church" pitch. Why? Simply put, we thought it would be refreshing for non-Christians to hear the pastor of a local church encouraging them to just do something specific to make their lives better. Of course, the best life is most truly developed by a relationship with

Christ, but that part can come later. That piece needs more explaining and will only make sense to non-Christians as they learn more. We need to speak about things that they can understand in order to get them listening. The cultural wall has to be breached.

Advertising on a secular station costs more because it reaches more people, but that's the point—to reach people, especially those who aren't saved. We need to be involved with Christian broadcasting, but when we advertise on secular stations, we reach both Christian and secular audiences. I think advertising within the Christian community has its place, but I don't think it should be the primary way we reach new people for our churches. An ad on the religion page will help a few people who are looking for special events or would like to find a new church home, but it doesn't make much of a dent in our primary purpose.

Christians have built a cultural wall that non-Christians don't understand, so we need to overcome it as often as possible.

In nations where the gospel is just now being received, novel approaches are being used. Samaritan's Purse helps people by providing medical care and personal packages that provide help to families. That makes the group relevant and appreciated by the people they are serving, which often leads those helped to ask why. The answer to their question is the gospel.

The Salvation Army has demonstrated the value of leaping the cultural wall for years. Virtually everyone exposed to The Salvation Army values their work regardless of their faith position, but the eventual result of the Army's work is the presentation of the gospel.

Youth With A Mission has more people on the mission front than any other single missions-sending agency in the world. They start businesses to help nationals create wealth and provide the goods and services they need. They provide teachers, doctors, and builders to those in need. Their workforce is trained in everything from drama to economics. Why? The gospel.

We can minister Christ and His Word if we will be consumed in serving others rather than concerned with the supremacy of any particular method or ministry name. With two billion people on Earth who don't know about redemption through Christ, everyone of us has to reach as far as we can with the resources God has given us to touch those outside our cultural circles.

LET THE PRESS HELP YOU OVER THE WALL

Several years ago it dawned on us that there is a huge news media business that has an endless craving for stories. We first realized it when we saw how the Clinton campaign mastered the use of the news media. I had our staff read George Stephanopoulos' book *All Too Human*, and we learned some big ideas about developing relationships with the news media. I differ with George politically, but his ability to work the press for the Clinton campaign forever altered the way people deal with the press. After reading George's book, we started doing events with the news media in mind. Why? Because the media need news, and we want to speak to the people who watch the news. We stopped being defensive and cautious with the press, and we began being proactive. When something was buzzing in town, we would issue a press statement or a position paper.

Now, the press knows that by calling us they will always get a thoughtful, immediate response. We've done this as a church for years, and now we do it with the NAE. Even though our local church and the NAE have relatively small budgets for this type of thing, we are often given opportunities to speak to large secular audiences.

There are some elements of godliness that would be wrong to talk about publicly without being asked (prayer, giving, and so on), but there are other elements of our work that communicate our message when covered by the news, such as our love for people and our desire to serve them. Those issues need to be communicated across the cultural wall in a way that makes sense. The news does that for us.

THE PROACTIVE MESSAGE LEAPS OVER THE CULTURAL WALL

When we're advertising, we need to make sure we are following the main principle of this chapter: promoting Christ is more important than promoting our particular method. In fact, promoting ourselves over other churches can do great harm to the gospel. *Comparative* advertising encourages Christians to go from one church to the other. *Proactive* advertising brings the gospel to unsaved people.

A pastor friend told me that his church's promotional materials were already proactive. "Well, let's look at them," I said.

He spent his entire promotional budget on Christian radio and television. His television ads said that his church offered "exciting services with practical, relevant Bible teaching."

Since he placed these ads on Christian television, he was really saying, "My church is more exciting than the one you go to," which is an encouragement to leave your church and begin attending his. If he placed these ads on secular radio, he would need to explain what "exciting services" means, since most non-Christians can't even imagine what they view as "exciting" going on inside a church.

He also said that the church offered "practical, relevant Bible teaching" without realizing that this implies that the teaching of other churches is inferior. Furthermore, are secular people looking for "practical, relevant Bible teaching"? No, they're looking for purpose in their lives, answers to their problems at work, and ways to keep their families together.

, , , , ,

When we reach the world, we also reach the church. If we target those already in church, we are, in effect, tempting Christians to become disgruntled.

, , , , ,

Churches who promote themselves should focus on the absolutes. That way, when Christians from Bible-believing churches hear a radio ad, for example, they will be edified. And when non-Christians hear the ad, they will be encouraged to trust the Lord and His Word. The name of the sponsoring church should be mentioned but not emphasized—because it is not the point.

An example of proactive advertising is this ad that New Life Church ran on several different secular radio stations, including country music and hard rock stations.

I know you're busy trying to get ready for work and get the kids off to school, but I just wanted to encourage you to read your Bible for just a minute or two before you leave for work this morning. Hi, my name is Ted Haggard, and I serve as the senior pastor at New Life Church up on the north side of Colorado Springs. And I just want to remind you that the Bible includes great information on how to have a successful marriage, how to raise children, how to have a successful career, and even how to balance your budget. The Bible will help your relationship with your supervisor, your co-workers, and (slight chuckle) with God. So trust me: If you'll invest just a few minutes in reading your Bible before you leave your house this morning, you're going to have a better day for it. The Bible has been a trusted companion for people for thousands of years. It's been a comfort and a help to people in all types of economic situations and all types of relational dilemmas. In order for us to be successful in life, we've got to add value to ourselves every day. That means we need to have better ideas today than we did yesterday. And how do we do that? By reading our Bible.

No one cares about my face or what my church looks like. I cannot meet their needs—only Jesus can. I as the pastor am a signpost to point people to Christ, so I am not the person to be promoted. Only Jesus offers everlasting comfort and healing; His Word provides the direction.

When we reach the world, we also reach the church. If we target those already in church, we are, in effect, tempting Christians to become disgruntled. Christians will compare ministries to decide where they want to worship and what ministries they want to support. We don't want too much of this, even though it does provide Christian leaders with market signals so they can keep their ministries improving. But our outreach dollars should not be spent convincing Christians that our ministry is better. Instead, it should be spent reaching those who don't know the lordship of Christ.

Most churches and pastors would never consciously promote a person instead of the gospel. But it often happens in the way the church presents itself to the public. The key is to focus on the absolutes instead of the church or pastor.

New Life Church also did some proactive promotion on billboards and bus signs. On the next page are examples of those signs. Notice how the message is "Jesus," while the name of the church is presented inconspicuously.

SECULAR MEDIA

While I was a young youth pastor at Bethany World Prayer Center in Baker, Louisiana, I scheduled a rock music seminar. On the night of the seminar, the building was full, the parking lot was gridlocked, and cars were backed up for two miles in three directions trying to get in. *CBS Evening News* taped the church's activities, interviewed students and adults, and collected sound bytes for the evening news. Why? Because the Peters Brothers were giving a rock music seminar.

What? Since when did that kind of thing attract so much attention?

When I scheduled the seminar with the Peters Brothers, we decided to promote the multimedia event among the people who enjoyed rock music the most. We paid to have the top rock disk jockeys make spots that offered the secrets to the lyrics and music of the most popular groups. The top rock stations ran advertisements inviting people to attend.

Many students from local public schools responded, and many came to Christ that night. Even students who weren't Christians stopped listening to secular rock and started buying Christian tapes for their vehicles. The gospel message had effectively penetrated the cultural wall; the lives of thousands of students were transformed. *CBS Evening News* even thought it newsworthy!

Sometimes we wonder why the secular news media never cover our major Christian events. We are tempted to believe that it is because of an anti-Christian bias. I don't think so. I think it is because our events don't touch their world.

Several years ago, the debate surrounding Colorado's Amendment 2 gave Colorado Springs the opportunity to communicate the gospel on the other side of the cultural wall. Bill Moyers, NBC, National Public Radio, the British Broadcasting Corporation (BBC), the International News Network, and numerous newspapers interviewed me

Illustration 2

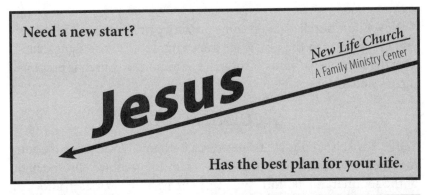

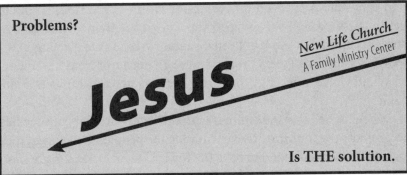

and other Christians about the growth of the Christian community in our city.

The news crews who came to tape these spots were amazed at New Life Church. Understand, New Life Church is a very typical, independent charismatic church. It has lively worship, strong teaching, and altar ministry. These reporters, though, had never seen anything like it. NBC called it a phenomenon. BBC said they were sure there wasn't another group like it in the world. They, obviously, were very wrong. But in their worldview there was no such thing as a culturally relevant group of believers. Why? Because the church has not penetrated their world.

The cultural wall must be penetrated. We must be in the world. Our message is for them.

So we buy thirty-second radio or television spots and place proactive advertisements on secular programming. We try to place some spots on the filthiest programs we can find. Occasionally, though, we also advertise on children's programs, sports, or news programs.

Though we have used television spots that certain Christian ministries have made for churches to use as an evangelistic tool from time to time, we also produce some of our own spots. One we did in the early years was filmed in a bar and titled "No More Lonely Nights." One couple saw this spot while they were watching television together in a bar.

"I hate that spot," the man joked with his date.

"I do, too," she replied.

But within a few weeks they ended up at New Life Church and gave their lives to Christ. Now the husband is our Promise Keepers ministry coordinator! If that spot had not been on a secular television program being aired in a bar, we would not have had access to this couple, because they were living on the other side of the cultural wall.

Recently, one of my associates, Rob Brendle, developed a relationship with one of the writers for a liberal independent newspaper here called the *Toilet Paper*. Part of the mission of the paper is to critique strong religious voices—one of the regular features is a picture of a ninja kicking a different church each week. After some negative press from that paper, Rob called the publisher and invited him to lunch.

By the end of the lunch, the publisher asked Rob to become a regular columnist! Rob now writes a column for those searching for spiritual truths titled "Soul Search." What an opportunity to cross the cultural wall and speak some truth to those who would probably never come searching for it at church!

Stop Keeping Count

Remember the *JESUS* video project? Some years ago, ninety-six different churches went around Colorado Springs giving away videotapes about Jesus. Some pastors wanted to figure out how many new people came to their churches because of their effort. I had no idea. But I knew my church was growing.

So was Woodman Valley Chapel.

And Village Seven Presbyterian.

And Briargate Baptist, and hundreds of other local churches.

In fact, I'm glad no one could say how many new people came to any particular church from that effort. Because if we just counted people in our own churches, we missed the point. I could tell, however, that where we prayed and distributed videos, Christian activity increased across the board.

In other words, we could see that Christ and His Word had been promoted. But we couldn't break it down into particular mission or methods. That project was about promoting Christ, not ourselves, and it resulted in obvious growth within the kingdom of God in Colorado Springs.

That's called raising the "water level" of the Holy Spirit's activity in your city, and I'll tell you exactly how it works in the next chapter.

SIX

PRAY TO RAISE THE "WATER LEVEL" OF THE HOLY SPIRIT'S ACTIVITY IN YOUR CITY

(PRINCIPLE #3)

I N THE SAME way that water levels in a reservoir change according to the time of year or amount of rainfall, so cities and regions experience varying levels of the Holy Spirit's activity.

One indication of the Holy Spirit's activity is an increase in the number of active Christians in an area. When a Christian is active, he or she will attend a church. Therefore, we can measure the "water level" of the Holy Spirit's activity in a city by looking at the percentage of people who are attending church on an average Sunday morning.

I used to say we needed to measure the level of Holy Spirit activity by the number of people attending a life-giving church on an average Sunday morning. But that forced people to differentiate between life-giving and non-life-giving churches in their regions, which is tricky. So, in order to measure the water level of the Holy Spirit's activity, we observe the number of people attending any Christian church on an average weekend (also accounting for the growing popularity of Saturday night services). At the same time, we encourage all Christians to do everything they can to make all churches life giving.

If 10 percent of your city's population is in church on an average weekend, you could graph the water level at 10 percent. By praying to increase the water level of the Holy Spirit's activity in your city by 1 percent in the next year, you would be praying for the Holy Spirit to draw, save, and fill an additional 1 percent of the people in your city, bringing the water level to 11 percent.

Colorado Springs has a population of approximately four hundred thousand, and there are about four hundred churches in the area. In order to raise the water level 1 percent in a year, four thousand more people would need to attend church. That is an average growth of ten people in each of the four hundred churches. That is possible!

We can also measure the water level of the Holy Spirit's activity in cities and in nations. Some nations we can measure in regions within a nation. The reason we need to measure is so that we can know which direction the activity of the Holy Spirit is moving in a city, region, or nation and so that we can know where to put our resources. Strategically targeting the darkest areas of our darkest cities and nations is the key to advancing the Great Commission. And it is helpful to measure trends so we can ensure continued growth. Otherwise we won't know where we are or how we're doing.

SPHERES OF INFLUENCE

The squares in Illustration 3 on the next page represent your city. In City A, the circles represent the spheres of influence of a local church. Among the non-Christian citizens in your city, those inside the spheres of influence have greatest access to the gospel message. The space between the spheres of influence represents the people in the community that do not have easy access to a personal gospel witness.

City B demonstrates what would happen if your particular church tripled in the next year. Although a 300 percent growth rate would be remarkably impressive, note that it doesn't make a major difference in the number of people who can hear the gospel message citywide. One church experiencing phenomenal growth does not make it that much harder to go to hell from your city.

But City C demonstrates the effect of a group of churches doubling their spheres of influence. When that happens, the area outside the influence of the gospel message becomes dramatically smaller. When this type of growth occurs, newly planted churches greatly assist the

Illustration 3

INCREASING THE INFLUENCE
OF THE CHURCH IN A CITY

CITY A

Most of the population lives outside the influence of any church.

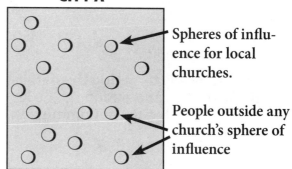

Spheres of influence for local churches.

People outside any church's sphere of influence

CITY B

Growth in only one church leaves much of the city still unreached.

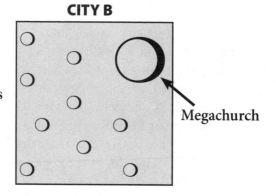

Megachurch

CITY C

Growth in all churches makes it difficult to avoid the gospel.

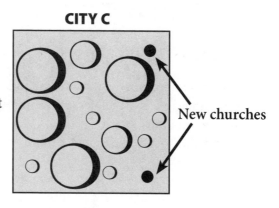

New churches

preexisting churches in reaching areas of the community still beyond their spheres of influence. A few years of broad-based church growth is the only way I know of to make it hard to go to hell from your city and create the societal shifts necessary to reflect a widespread gospel impact.

, , , , ,

Strategically targeting the darkest areas of our darkest cities and nations is the key to advancing the Great Commission.

, , , , ,

Again, church growth across a group of churches is the best way to make it hard to go to hell from your city.

Now that we have been doing this for so many years, we have started to see which patterns work and which ones don't. In cities that have been clearly impacted by the gospel, the transition happened both because of the planting and/or development of new local churches and citywide networking among disparate churches. If the Assemblies of God churches or the Baptist churches work with just their own constituency, it doesn't make a citywide or regional impact. Why? Because there is not a broad enough diversity in the churches that are reaching out. But if the Assemblies of God churches, the Baptist churches, the Mennonite churches, and various other types of churches in the city all work together, the likelihood of measurable impact dramatically increases because they can appeal to a great diversity of people.

So, in order to raise the water level of the Holy Spirit's activity in your city or region, it is imperative to build a team of churches from various streams.

PRAYER PROMOTES GROWTH

Additionally, it is important to be strategic about prayer. In fact, to get any real work done in city strategies, prayer is foundational—we can't get anywhere without it.

When I pray and fast, I like to rent a room with a couple of friends in an area where we can go on prayer walks through neighborhoods. Our goal is to raise the water level of the Holy Spirit's activity in that section of the city. As we walk through the neighborhood praying, we pray for the people who live in the homes we pass by. We pray for the businesses we come across and for God's blessing on every church we walk past.

We sometimes don't know anything specific about the churches we come across, so we pray in a way that we would appreciate others praying for us. We walk around the church asking God to bless all of those who worship there. We war against any demonic spirits working against the church or the individuals who attend. We ask God to bless them financially, encourage their vision, increase their passion, and add more families to their church body.

We take oil, as a symbol of the Holy Spirit, and place it at the corners of the church buildings. We anoint the perimeter of the property. We stand as intercessors, asking God for great miracles.

If we happen to know that the church we are praying for is not evangelical, we become aggressive for God's blessing. We pray for the revelation of Scripture and the power of the Holy Spirit to be manifest in these churches. We pray for a personal encounter with the Lord that will change them into churches with core beliefs in the Bible as God's Word and Jesus as God's Son.

We are always careful not to draw attention to ourselves or to appear threatening. If we feel awkward, we'll just pray discreetly while walking by the front of the church at a normal pace. Our purpose is not to be seen but to increase the water level of the Holy Spirit's activity in the region. Prayer stimulates the Holy Spirit's activity.

On Friday nights, we have a group of well-trained intercessors who pray in local churches throughout Colorado Springs. Pastors will unlock their front doors and allow the team to walk through their building soaking it in prayer. We pray for the congregation to experience the power of God and for the pastor to be rejuvenated. The team often also walks through the neighborhood and prays. They pray for the surrounding area to grow spiritually thirsty and start attending that local church.

Illustration 4

A Measure of the Water Level of the Holy Spirit's Activity in a City

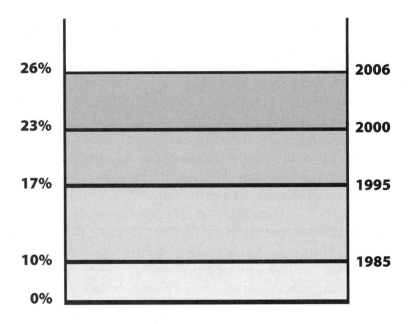

The percentage of a city's population in
church on a Sunday morning

As in 1985, the rumor was that about 10 percent of our city attended church on an average weekend. Then prayer teams started aggressively praying over our city. According to some of the information gathered by the Colorado Springs Association of Evangelicals, we estimate that 17 percent of the population of Colorado Springs attended church on an average weekend by 1995. In 2000, one survey said that 23 percent of the city was attending church on an average weekend, and now we believe a little more than 26 percent of our city attends church on an average weekend. By Bible-belt standards, we have a long way to go, but we're moving in the right direction.

This illustrates the importance of having some reasonably accurate statistics in order to know where we are and what direction we are moving. And, when we know numbers like this, we know where to fund mission projects, where to plant churches, and where to go on prayer journeys. I don't think the numbers need to be perfect by a researcher's standards. I think that we just need to be familiar with the general trajectory of the spiritual climate of the region.

When we start to pray in terms of raising the water level, it confuses demonic resistance and opens the door to greater manifestations of God's kingdom. It also helps us realize that other people's successes are not a threat because, as the water level increases in the region, our own ministries will increase as well. It's obviously a win-win situation.

BUBBLES OF CHURCH GROWTH

Numbers from the 1980s and 1990s are forcing us to rethink growth in the church.

During that time, we in America experienced the phenomenal growth of the megachurches and the large parachurch ministries. (The standard for a megachurch is a church that has a regular attendance of two thousand or more.) As churches and ministries were growing, we thought that the gospel message was reaching a greater percentage of people. Unfortunately, after looking a little closer, it turned out that even though megachurches were indeed growing and parachurch ministries were expanding, we actually had a smaller percentage of the population involved in church and declaring themselves Christians than before. In many places, overall church attendance was declining.

A megachurch is like a bubble or a wave in the water level of a community. (See Illustration 5 on page 64.)

In order to sustain a bubble like this over time, the water level around the bubble needs to be increased.

It takes a tremendous amount of energy to maintain a bubble over an extended period of time. In many cases, the bubble churches of one decade become the average churches of the next.

In addition to spending the energy necessary to expand a large

Illustration 5

A BUBBLE IN THE
WATER LEVEL OF A CITY

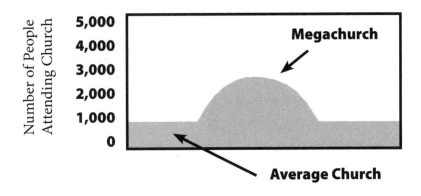

church, we need to do everything we can to raise the water level around the bubble, thus allowing it to stay large with greater ease, or become an even larger church. But to try to make the church larger without raising the entire water level in the community can be difficult.

For example, right now in Colorado Springs, New Life Church is disproportionately larger than most other churches in the region. I want New Life Church to grow even larger because of the reality of heaven and hell. But to embrace the overall growth of the kingdom in our region, we must encourage other churches in the region to grow.

If a city has several churches with a Sunday attendance of three thousand, then a bubble of a church of six thousand on Sundays could be sustained. But if the other large churches have only five hundred people, it would be difficult for one church to maintain a consistent Sunday attendance of six thousand.

A couple of years ago, an articulate young pastor told me he desired to start a new church in Colorado Springs. Far too many pastors become nervous in that situation, but heaven and hell are in the balance. I believe every life-giving church in our city is a blessing from

God. So I told the pastor that he would be smart to plant his church as close to New Life Church as possible. Why? So he could get the overflow. Currently, his congregation meets just down the road and is thriving! I desire for that church to grow stronger and become a life-giving force in our city.

New Life performs an Easter production with hundreds of people in the cast. Around our church, Easter is the most exciting time of the year. Last year, we had 49,123 people come through our building to see the story of Jesus. Of those, 4,372 made first-time commitments to Christ. That is a wonderful number, and it is more new people than we are equipped to handle right now. In order to effectively disciple those people, there must be numerous growing churches in our city, not just ours.

Considering the position I'm in, I'm obviously an advocate for mega-churches. God is blessing the Christian community with megachurches and large parachurch ministries because He loves the lost. Mega-churches have a great accumulation of resources and prayer power that could transform cities—if their people don't make one crucial mistake.

THE ROLE OF THE MEGACHURCHES

We need more megachurches. With more than six billion people on the planet, we need as many large churches as possible. No doubt, we'll experience a proliferation of megachurches throughout the balance of our lives. But megachurches must be careful not to be deceived into thinking their growth means impact if, in reality, their resources become diluted. Let me illustrate.

As a church grows, decisions have to be made about the most effective ways to spend money to reach people. The budgets of most large local churches go toward buildings and staff. If excessive debt or exorbitant salaries don't become a problem, churches also have the opportunity to decide how to spend money on outreach.

At New Life Church we have made fundamental decisions about our outreach resources:

1. To concentrate our resources to produce measurable results for the kingdom of God in our region

2. To finance mission projects that raise the water level of the Holy Spirit's activity in dark areas of the world

Many churches make a major mistake by investing all their outreach money on nationwide programs that primarily minister to and reinforce an existing Christian culture. That investment will not have a concentrated impact on any one geographical area and probably won't make any measurable difference. Because these churches get some response, they know they are reaching and helping people. But they may be contributing to the fact that their own city is declining spiritually.

A pastor could take $35,000 per month and buy national radio or television time. Or a church could invest the same $35,000 in their region for communicating the gospel through local media and community service.

, , , , ,

Many churches make a major mistake by investing all their outreach money on nationwide programs that primarily minister to and reinforce an existing Christian culture.

, , , , ,

In the first scenario the pastor may become well known and could demonstrate success by increased income, growing mailing lists, and additional opportunities—all producing wonderful testimonial letters. But, in the midst of a growing ministry, it is doubtful that the church could point to any specific city where its influence contributed to a measurable decline in crime rates, growth in overall church attendance, or any other societal adjustment.

Instead of investing heavily in media time, we invest in projects that make life better for individuals in our city. As a result, there are some projects that the media identify as noteworthy. Personally, I have found the secular media in Colorado Springs to be a friend. That may sound strange to people who shun the media, but as I said earlier, I believe the local media can be a great asset in reaching our cities for the kingdom.

When we invest in reaching our cities, we increase our opportunity to make a measurable impact in a specific area. A megachurch will make a lasting impact if it puts definite geographical boundaries on its ministry. When we maintain boundaries, we accumulate water and have a massive reservoir of strength with which to communicate the gospel to everyone in our population area. But, as with a dam, if the boundaries aren't there, the water becomes shallow, and the impact is diluted.

TRANSFER OR CONVERSION GROWTH

Transfer growth occurs when people move from one church to another but make no overall improvement in the water level of the Holy Spirit's activity in a city. (See Illustration 6 on page 68.) The only positive impact of transfer growth is when a person switches from a nonbelieving church to a life-giving church. Sometimes transfer growth occurs when Christians move into town and are looking for a new church home. At other times, however, another church may not have adequately met their felt needs, so they choose to switch churches.

Some pastors feel that if the church they pastor is growing, the city must be becoming more Christian. The reality is that if one church grows because another is declining, then there is no net difference in the social and cultural makeup of the city.

Conversion growth is much more difficult, but it makes an immediate improvement in the water level of the Holy Spirit's activity in a city. It requires reaching into the nonchurched community with the gospel message and discipling those who respond to the Lord.

If we focus on transfer growth in our prayers, thoughts, and actions, we focus on ourselves. We pray, think, and act in terms of self-preservation and self-promotion. Comparative thinking and speaking become the norm.

Illustration 6

A Church Focused
on Transfer Growth

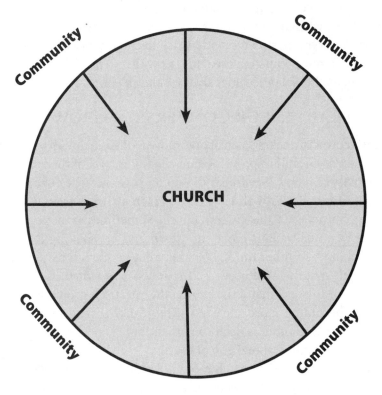

**The church focuses on itself, and the
community receives little attention.**

In contrast, people in churches that emphasize conversion growth intentionally focus on serving and encouraging the unchurched. Proactive and creative thinking and praying are required for conversion growth. Attention is focused on the larger community. (See Illustration 7.)

Some transfer growth will occur as a natural by-product of working for conversion growth. Transfer growth can be a healthy and necessary development, but it cannot be the focus of our efforts.

On an average Sunday morning, half the congregation at New Life Church is made up of transfers from other churches, and the other half is people who were either born again or have recommitted their lives to Christ in our church. That means we have made a legitimate

Illustration 7

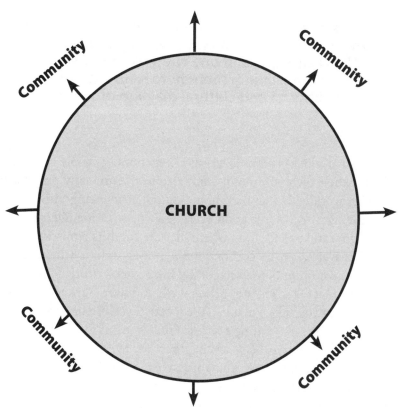

A CHURCH FOCUSED ON CONVERSION GROWTH

The church focuses on the community, not itself.

contribution to raising the water level of the Holy Spirit's activity in our city. If our church was comprised predominantly of transfer members, it would indicate that we hadn't made a significant difference in the social or cultural balance of Colorado Springs.

My job right now is to do all I can to encourage the growth of other life-giving churches in our region and to raise the water level of the Holy Spirit's activity in Colorado Springs. As this happens, all of us grow, we have greater opportunities, and our city is effectively reached for the cause of the kingdom.

＞＞＞＞＞

Some pastors feel that if the church they pastor is growing, the city must be becoming more Christian. The reality is that if one church grows because another is declining, then there is no net difference in the social and cultural makeup of the city.

＞＞＞＞＞

Now that global prayer is so easy, I encourage people not only to pray for their own community, but also to intentionally pray for the churches worldwide that their home church is financing through missions giving. I think it is good every few years for members of every church to travel to a location where they are funding a mission church and to prayer walk the community. A prayer walk is when we walk through a community praying for it. I have a book entitled *Taking It to the Streets* that details how to prayer walk. A prayer journey is the same thing, except you take a plane to the location you are praying for.

Right now we are sending a series of prayer teams to Pakistan to pray with a pastor who has been serving there for over forty years. We are also sending teams to Iraq, Afghanistan, Israel, the Gaza Strip, and various other key places in the world. Prayer teams in North Korea, China, Vietnam, Cuba, and other key locations are very important. And for those who don't want to take risks, cities like London, New York, Washington DC, Tokyo, Cairo, and others are in desperate need. Always serve the local churches as you go, and you will see great results.

A few years ago we decided to multiply specific prayers through the use of the Internet. We all know that every prayer matters to God and that we have increased strength when we pray together. With this in mind, we began a real-time prayer meeting on the Web (www .worldprayerteam.org). People from all over the world log on to spend time praying for focused prayer targets. At this writing, there are typically 70,000 people at this site worldwide praying for requests as they come in. It's the largest continuous prayer meeting in the world—all online. When someone gets onto the site, they are able to see world events and personal prayer requests that need prayer, and they can distribute their prayer request to intercessors all over the world.

I have received phone calls and e-mails from people all over the world who have seen a measurable change in their situation simply because people prayed. Miracles have happened in the midst of natural and man-made disasters. Young children have been healed. Family members have come to Christ. Marriages have been rescued. Our prayers matter to God, and He delights in answering them.

When we pray to raise the water level of the Holy Spirit's activity in our city, many times we end up praying for ministries that interpret some portions of Scripture differently than we do or have a different culture from ours. But they are still part of the body of Christ. Therefore, as we will explore in the next chapter, we must appreciate one another's respected interpretations of Scripture and learn to view our differences as a strength.

—SEVEN—

APPRECIATE ONE ANOTHER'S RESPECTED INTERPRETATIONS OF SCRIPTURE

(PRINCIPLE #4)

URING WORLD WAR II some soldiers had a buddy who died. They went to a local Roman Catholic parish and asked the priest if they could bury their friend in the fenced graveyard beside the church.

The old priest asked, "Was the man Roman Catholic?"

"We haven't any idea," they said.

The priest replied, "Well, you'll have to bury him just outside the graveyard fence then."

So they buried the body outside the fence and left. They happened to pass through the same town later, however, and visited their friend's grave. They looked at the fence in amazement. It wasn't where it had been before. The old priest, realizing that his way of thinking was ungodly, had moved the fence to include the fallen soldier's grave.

ENLARGING YOUR TERRITORY

In this story, the priest's territory was enlarged once he decided to include the fallen soldier. It's the same way with you and me. As we focus on the absolutes and work with our brothers and sisters from differing denominations or affiliations, God is able to expand our territory, and thus we are able to reach more people for the kingdom of God.

The issue with appreciating one another's respected interpretations is that humility is a precursor. We must prioritize our beliefs and activities and be willing to accept the reality of absolutes in contrast to the interpretation, deductions, and preferences that we embrace. The cause of Christ has more depth, understanding, and purpose than our own movements within the body of Christ. The truth is, Jesus, the head of the church, uses those differences to reach the lost. Our distinctives are not a failure of unity, but rather they are an evidence that we are, in fact, a family, a body, and building put together by God Himself. And, as a result, our differences are our strength, designed by God to make all of us in His body more effective.

I LOVE ICE CREAM STORES

I love all kinds of ice cream. Sometimes I want vanilla with caramel topping, whipped cream, lots of nuts, and a cherry. Other times I want rocky road, banana, or chocolate chip. Very seldom do I like plain vanilla, but sometimes perky strawberry sounds good.

That's why I love the Baskin-Robbins ice cream stores. They have thirty-one flavors, and I can always find something I like. All of it is ice cream, but each has a different flavor.

, , , , ,

Where the church is growing most rapidly, there is a strong emphasis on many kinds of local churches being effective within the community. These places (consciously or unconsciously) utilize the diversity of the body instead of resenting it or preventing it, and everyone is strengthened.

, , , , ,

In Colorado Springs we enjoy ninety different flavors of churches. Most of these groups stand on the message of Christ as their cornerstone and embrace the Bible as their authority. So in each of them you could discover the same basic truths that make eternal life available to all.

By discussing various flavors in the body of Christ, I am not speaking of a totally ecumenical, humanistic movement that embraces all people of all faiths as brothers and sisters. I am saying that we need to appreciate one another's "respected interpretations" of Scripture, which are interpretations that are appreciated by mainstream evangelical biblical scholarship. These are not heresies or teachings that threaten the divinity of Christ or the integrity of His Word.

This idea really boils down to a free-market philosophy. Free markets force people to provide something of value to someone else before they are rewarded. It is inherently a system that forces everyone to serve others. As a result, there is a continuous competition to outserve, resulting in a steady stream of newly developed choices. With choice comes positive competition—the type of competition that requires improvement on everyone's part in order to stay competitive. And, of course, these improvements result in better products and services for everyone.

There are several reasons why the body of Christ is growing most rapidly in Asian Pacific Rim countries, Central and South America, and Africa. There are also reasons why the American church has transitioned from being dominated by liberalism to evangelicalism, which positions it for rapid growth, while at the same time the European church is in decline. Since Britain has the Church of England, Germany has the Lutheran Church, and Ukraine has the Russian Orthodox Church, the body of Christ in those nations is kept from having to be effective because when government endorses one particular church, others are viewed with suspicion, which limits positive competitive forces. The clergy earns what it earns whether it touches people's lives or not. But where the church is growing most rapidly, there is a strong emphasis on many kinds of local churches being effective within the community. These places (consciously or unconsciously) utilize the diversity of the body instead of resenting it or preventing it, and everyone is strengthened.

When we work together at offering the same life-changing message of Jesus Christ through different flavors, more lives are touched and more souls saved. Our primary purpose does not require every church to reach every person. That would be impossible. God has never used any one denomination of the church to reach everybody. It violates His establishment of the body. God requires specific groups to reach specific people effectively and helps us understand that a different flavor in the body of Christ is our co-worker to reach still another group. Through the strength we draw from our different flavors, we can communicate to the various people within our communities. I think it's clear: the Lord planned for local churches to be distinctive, because it gives us nuance, flexibility, and a greater reach.

REACHING THE LOST

Let's say that on Elm Street, USA, there are five Christian churches. Let's also assume each of the pastors has elected to focus on the absolutes of Scripture. One is Presbyterian, another Baptist, another Catholic, and another charismatic, and the last one is Methodist.

Joe Schmoe, a nonbeliever, moved to town and heard people speaking positively about the Lord in public. He decided to visit a church. Remember: Joe is a nonbeliever. He is not church-hopping or trying to find a church that will meet his emotional and cultural needs. He is searching for answers. All of our cities are full of people like Joe.

He began by attending the Presbyterian church. Everyone was dressed very nicely and was very polite. Hymns were sung, the choir was impressive, and the pastor explained that Jesus Christ is the only solution to mankind's sin problem. Joe heard the message and enjoyed the service but was a little uncomfortable with the formality.

The next Sunday he visited the charismatic church. Everyone was happy, loud, and direct. Music was playing, colors were bright, and the pastor was out in the crowd talking and laughing. When the service began, Joe was completely disoriented. People clapped their hands and jumped with joy. It was a wonderful celebration. But he had no idea how the people knew when to lift their hands and close their eyes or clap and jump.

When the pastor spoke, he explained the same basic principle the Presbyterian pastor explained: Jesus is the solution to mankind's sin problem. Joe enjoyed the church very much but didn't feel secure. He wanted something that felt a little more traditional.

The next week he moved on to the Catholic church and attended

Mass. The priest at this particular Catholic church was an evangelical; he encouraged his parishioners in their personal prayer lives and devotion to the Scriptures. As the priest delivered the homily, Joe heard about the powerful inner transformation available through a personal encounter with Christ. He heard, once again, about sins being forgiven. But even though the message spoke to him, the culture of the service was a stumbling block to him. He needed something much more relaxed.

The following Sunday, Joe visited the Methodist church. The Sunday school teacher told the story about going on a prayer journey into the 10/40 Window. She recited the events of powerful prayer and engaging intercession. She wanted to begin prayer walks in the community to raise the water level of the Holy Spirit's activity so that more people would experience the love of Jesus in their lives.

Joe's heart was touched. Rather than going to the main worship service, he stayed after the Sunday school class. He prayed with the teacher to accept Christ, and today Joe is a Spirit-filled Methodist.

How did that happen?

He heard the same basic message from the various flavors in the body of Christ. No one tried to convince him that his or her flavor was the perfect flavor able to meet every need. Instead, all of the flavors, while maintaining their own distinctives, communicated the necessity of Christ.

THE NEED FOR OTHERS

Several years ago we started to notice several families leaving our church and going to Woodmen Valley Chapel, a fine church located a few miles south of New Life. When most of these people left, they didn't say anything. Others told me how much they loved me as their pastor and appreciated New Life Church, but they felt led by the Lord to start attending Woodmen Valley Chapel. I couldn't understand what was going on. So I called my friend, Jim Tomberlin, who pastored Woodmen Valley. I told him about the trend, which of course he had also noticed, and asked him to listen for me to find out the real reason for the trend.

A couple of weeks later Jim called me back. He said the problem was our children's department. He said the word in the hallways was that the New Life system was horrible and practically impossible to navigate. It wasn't friendly; it wasn't helpful. It was so negative that even though people appreciated the rest of the church, our children's department overwhelmed the other positive attributes of the church, and, as a result, families were leaving.

I thanked Jim and we went to work. We had received the market signal, and we found the problem. Woodmen had a better children's department than we did, so we focused on improving ours. Positive competition helped us make a better hamburger, so to speak. Over the next few months, because of improvements in the children's department, our church and, of course, the children's ministry itself grew rapidly.

So, here we have it. New Life Church has grown because of our friendship with Woodmen Valley Chapel. They are very different than we are, but we learned some things from them that improved our ministry to children. With this kind of thinking, ministry city-wide can be continually improving as we observe our weak areas of ministry and improve them.

I often tell my staff the only way to improve is to watch those who are doing things better than we are and integrate their methods into our ministries. I don't encourage learning from those who don't know how to do effective ministry (and, unfortunately, some of the people who talk a lot about local church ministry have no track record of success in their own ministries). But those who do it better than we do it are wonderful teachers for all of us. As a result, we send our hospitality team to churches like Willow Creek Community Church and Phoenix First Assembly to learn new techniques in serving people through facilities management. Our college team visits North Point Community Church to gather new ideas and tactics to help provide better discipleship and create growth. All of these churches are outside of our theological stream. But without them, we may hit struggles or stagnate. In the body of Christ, we need each other.

Now we're in a situation where we can easily observe churches worldwide. As a result of the excellent work of so many of the brethren overseas, I now believe it's time for the American church leaders to become the students of some foreign church leaders. No one in the world has built a church and university like Bishop David Oyedepo in Lagos, Nigeria. We need to learn all we can from him. No one in the world has impacted a culture the way Pastor Sunday Adelaja has in Kiev, Ukraine. We need to learn all we can from him. No one has impacted a city the way Pastor Kong Hee has in Singapore. It would benefit all of us to study his work. And no one has renewed an existing church the way Brian Houston has in Sydney, Australia. We need to learn all we can from him.

These and so many others have done excellent work and not only need to be admired but also emulated. For the North American church to do what God has positioned us to do, we need to use our resources strategically and learn all we can from others in the body of Christ. Each of these men I've mentioned is in a different stream, but each is committed to the lordship of Jesus Christ, the integrity of the Scriptures, and the necessity of being born again. We are different than they are, but they are doing better work than many of us. Let's have an appreciation for one another's respected interpretations and open our hearts to learn so we can all be effective and make it harder to go to hell in our generation.

—EIGHT—

PRACTICE SUPPORTIVE SPEECH AND ACTIONS TOWARD OTHERS

(PRINCIPLE #5)

I N A SMALL town in Louisiana, I witnessed one of the finest examples of "supportive speech and action" I have ever seen.

A small downtown church had been in the community for years. Then a local Baptist pastor started a new church on the edge of the city, with very charismatic services.

As the Baptist church grew, the pastor of the smaller church was vehement. "There's a church on the other side of town full of false doctrine," he preached. "There are demonic things going on over there. Just stay away, because you never know what could happen to you."

But the Spirit-filled Baptists grew from one large building to an even larger one. Their youth group became bigger than the entire congregation at the other church. The downtown church pastor was more and more incensed, and he let everyone know it. The Baptist pastor never retaliated, and in fact always spoke highly of the way the pastor downtown had faithfully served the community.

This went on for fifteen years. As the smaller congregation continued to shrink, their little white frame building fell into disrepair. The Baptist church, on the other hand, was in well-maintained buildings and getting new, young families all the time.

Finally, the smaller church's building became unsafe. If they couldn't get the money to repair it, they would have to close. By this time, the congregation was down to thirty people. Money was scarce.

The pastor of the Baptist church heard about the problems of the church that had been preaching against him for so long. He immediately contacted the other pastor and explained that his church would like to help them. What did they need?

Within a month the Baptist church paid for the old church to be torn down. They soon built a brand-new brick building on the same spot for the body of elderly believers.

As you can imagine, that generous act changed the heart of the traditional pastor. He stopped preaching against the Baptist church even though they continued to be of a different flavor. He even started bragging about what good Christian people they were.

The body of Christ in the entire city was strengthened because of supportive speech and actions.

RESPECT SPIRITUAL AUTHORITY

When I first arrived in Colorado Springs, the potential existed for me to have my own standoff with a local pastor.

Just after my arrival, the Village Seven Presbyterian Church took a very public position regarding some of the loose theology taught in charismatic circles. This was a major blow to the smaller charismatic churches and to those who believed in the modern-day operation of the gifts.

About the time that announcement was made at Village Seven, we were a small storefront church, and God was dealing with me about spiritual authority. I had been reading Gene Edwards's *A Tale of Three Kings*, Watchman Nee's *Spiritual Authority*, and material from Bill Gothard. The ideas in the three combined resources made a huge impact on me.

As I prayed over the city, I received a strong impression that I had limited authority and that I needed to honor those in the city whom God had chosen to honor. I asked Him who the spiritual leaders of the city were, and Pastor Bernie Kuiper, the noncharismatic pastor of Village Seven Presbyterian Church, came to mind.

I made an appointment with Dr. Kuiper. When I met with him I explained that I believed he was chosen by God as a spiritual leader in the city and that I would always speak respectfully and honorably about him. He grilled me with several questions regarding charismatic theology and, I believe, was pleasantly surprised by my answers. To my surprise, when it was time to go he asked me to get on my knees in front of him. When I did, he placed his hands on my head and asked God to bless New Life Church and to make it the largest church in Colorado Springs. I would have never have asked for such a blessing, but God granted it, I think, because I assured Pastor Kuiper in the midst of our conversation that I would not do any ministry outside spiritual authority—which in my mind meant outside Pastor Kuiper's blessing. His prayer was answered.

Not long after that, volunteers from several churches met together at Radiant Assembly of God to organize a Christmas-season outreach through television and radio spots. We set up a phone bank at our church, and several churches from throughout the city volunteered to answer phones when people would call for prayer. Both Pastor Kuiper and I were there to speak and encourage people to participate. Instead of speaking one at a time, we stood at the front together and talked about how exciting it was to see new people come to Jesus.

I guess talking about so many people coming to Christ loosened us up a bit. Laughing, we agreed that if anyone went to Village Seven and got too emotional, Dr. Kuiper would send them to New Life. And if anyone came to New Life in a suit that cost more than fifteen hundred dollars, we would send them to Village Seven. The crowd laughed and applauded.

I think they loved seeing two pastors put aside their differences and work together for the spiritual health of a city. I have warmly referred to Pastor Kuiper as "bishop" ever since, and even though he is now retired, I always think of him with respect and fondness.

As I mentioned earlier, I now serve the NAE as president. I am able to perform that role because of my early positive experiences of working with so many flavors of the body of Christ in Colorado Springs. Our members are as diverse as can be, and sometimes the difference between denominations and congregations can seem overly important. If we are not careful to speak well of one another and actively serve one another, the differences could separate us rather than allowing us to draw on one another's strengths.

Actually, my role in the NAE is even more specifically related to this issue. When I was a new pastor in Colorado Springs, there were two groups of pastors who met on a regular basis, and I had to decide which one to meet with. One group was comprised of local charismatic pastors, which was a natural fit for me; the other group was comprised of several retired pastors making up the local chapter of the NAE, which was not my natural fit. But I attended the latter of the two. I am confident that I was the only person in that group under the age of sixty-five. Yet, somehow they saw fit to elect me, in my early thirties, as president of their little body. Then someone suggested that I attend the national convention. (I, of course, was not even aware that there was a national convention.) Again, I was one of the youngest people in the group by at least three decades—this time at the national convention of the NAE. I have served with the NAE from that time on, through its most difficult years and under several different presidencies. I served as an usher. I ran errands. I agreed to serve on the board, then the executive committee, and then was asked to serve as president.

Here is the point: I believe in respecting people. I don't serve the NAE because I want to be president. I serve it because I believe that united evangelical action is vitally necessary in our generation. I would serve in any role they asked me to, because I believe in the importance of diverse evangelicals working together.

IT DOESN'T HURT TO TALK

Years ago, Colorado Springs was in deep division because of Amendment 2, an amendment to the Colorado Constitution that would prevent anyone from bringing a claim of discrimination based on sexual orientation. Because of the hostility that developed in the midst of that debate, religious leaders decided to form a group so we could meet together to discuss issues affecting our community. The group was made up of our local rabbi; the Roman Catholic bishop; James Dobson from Focus on the Family; James White, the only pastor in town who, at that time, would do same-sex marriages; the mayor of the city, who attended First United Methodist; myself; and a few others.

This group no longer meets, but our time together allowed us to establish a foundation of respect. After a few months of meetings, we started to become friends. Our common ground is the fact that all of us worship the God of Israel and have a deep conviction that people should be both respectful and respected.

As a result, the group members signed a Covenant of Mutual Respect. We distributed it in our churches and printed it in the newspaper on a full-page ad so the community could see it. The second paragraph of the covenant reads:

> The diversity of our religious perspectives may lead us into areas of possible disagreement. It is our hope to address those areas of difference with an attitude of openness, respect and love, and a willingness to listen and learn from each other, to the end that we may manifest the ministry of reconciliation. With this hope and prayer before us, we covenant together to conduct our common life by the scriptural standards of justice, mercy, righteousness and peace as we provide leadership in our congregations, organizations and community. We believe that in so doing we reflect the nature of our God—the Creator of the universe and Lord of all!

This covenant has helped create close friendships among the groups. Now, whenever any of our organizations is involved in a major project, we have a friendly, supportive climate that allows for free, open discussions and security. To this day, those relationships serve the spiritual climate in Colorado Springs.

Colorado Springs is not perfect. We have many, many problems, just like any other city. But in the areas where we have connected and created valuable relationships, the spiritual life of our city is served in a positive way.

DARE TO LIKE PEOPLE
WITH WHOM YOU DISAGREE

I am not fearful of liking people who don't agree with me on everything.

In any free society, it is important for ideas to flow freely. I know the events of the gospel are the grandest events in history. I know there is

85

a God in heaven, and He has definite opinions. I also know that the people who live in our city believe what they believe for important reasons. And I should hear and understand those reasons. Very often, when I do that, I end up forming an unexpected friendship.

The Catholic Diocese of Colorado Springs hosted a Congress on Reconciliation, Healing, and Hospitality. We discussed the questions: "What drives us apart?" and "What brings us together?" The two guest speakers were Robert Bellah, author of *Habits of the Heart* and *The Good Society*, and Margaret O'Brien Steinfels, author of *Who's Minding the Children: The History and Politics of Day Care in America*, both social liberals.

To complement these major speakers was a panel of guest speakers from our community. They included Clair Garcia, an African American English professor from Colorado College; Howard Hirsch, rabbi of Temple Shalom and professor of religion at Regis College; Mary Lou Makepeace, the senior member of the Colorado Springs City Council; and me.

We represented a broad variety of responses to the presentations given by the main speakers. We attend different places of worship. We embrace different political positions. We have competing views on many social/political/spiritual issues—but we are all friends. We honestly enjoy and respect one another—we honor one another. We have the opportunity to communicate ideas to one another so that the Catholic community has a wholesome understanding of the heart of the conservative evangelical, and so on.

Sometimes even a blunt disagreement can be transformed into an opportunity to find common ground.

The months before the release of *The Passion of the Christ* were filled with media interviews. Often, of course, the media pitted conservative Christian views against liberal Jewish views. I debated several rabbis over the merits of the film on news networks like CNN.

During several of the debates, CNN juxtaposed me against Rabbi Hyre from the Simon Wiesenthal Center in Los Angeles. I know why CNN kept using him. He was a particularly articulate opponent, and our altercations would become quite energetic—it made for good entertainment news.

After one CNN debate, Rob Brendle, my associate I mentioned earlier, called Rabbi Hyre so I could talk with him. He dialed 411, got his office number in California, and two minutes later Rabbi Hyre's secretary patched me through to his cell phone. Through the conversation that followed, we were able to open communication and discuss how we could support one another on the matter.

In the end, the NAE and the Simon Wiesenthal Center made a united statement: "No matter what your opinion of *The Passion*, anti-Semitism and any other form of discrimination is wrong." Although I am personally supportive of *The Passion* and find no evidence of it being anti-Semitic, the body of Christ was glorified by this effort to work together. Rabbi Hyre and I have been warm friends and close allies ever since.

, , , , ,

Sometimes even a blunt disagreement can be transformed into an opportunity to find common ground.

, , , , ,

We need to reach out even to those from whom we appear to be miles apart. We need each other. We need to speak well of one another.

Some time ago, the front page of the Sunday morning paper had a huge color picture of me in our church auditorium. Above my head were three ten-by-ten-foot screens on which we project the words to our songs and our announcements. And on the screens were the names of each of our county commissioners. The headline over the article read "Religion and Politics."

The article never explained why the names of the county commissioners were on our projection screens. But it did talk in general terms about how religious organizations were influencing politics. So the impression was that I was a political activist and used the Sunday morning service to coach the congregation about our county commissioners.

But on that particular Sunday morning, we as a congregation were filling out our annual prayer guides. On one page of that prayer guide, we needed to fill in the names of the county commissioners, so I had arranged to have the names projected on the screen so that people could copy them down.

The minute that newspaper hit the streets, the newspaper offices started getting responses—first from people who had attended the service and knew what the names were there for, then from the people in town who had a relationship with me or the church. It was heartwarming when the Jewish community, the Catholic community, and the conservative and liberal Protestant community all defended New Life. They all communicated: "What you said about New Life was not true!"

A few days later, the newspaper printed a retraction.

In his new book *Winning With People*, John Maxwell discusses what he calls "The Number 10 Principle." Maxwell explains that as we lead people, the more we expect from and entrust to them, the more they will produce and flourish. If we treat them as if they are mature leaders, they will produce like mature leaders.

One day my associate senior pastor Ross Parsley and I were walking on the church grounds when we saw an unshaven, casually dressed man looking slightly puzzled by the schedule of prayer we keep on the wall of our World Prayer Center. We stopped and asked the man if we could help him find anything. He told us he was visiting the center to pray for a few days and was thinking of renting a hotel room nearby. After a brief introduction and a quick look around the building, we got him checked into one of the guest suites on campus and said good-bye.

A few days later both Ross and I received large personal checks in the mail from our new friend. He wrote each of us a note in which he thanked us for taking a couple of minutes to show him around and give him some encouragement. That man, who we later discovered is a wealthy businessman from Southern Colorado, has been one of the major donors in several New Life projects since then. It goes to show that even the most unexpected person might be a leader, so we better treat them like it.

EXERCISE WISDOM

Speaking respectfully and thoughtfully about others can never hurt us. Jack Hayford's attitude toward John MacArthur is a blessing to the body of Christ. (Jack is charismatic and John is anti-charismatic.) If Jack began saying negative things about John, the body of Christ would be hurt.

Now, I'm not saying we should be spineless creatures, fearful of taking strong positions. Neither Jack Hayford nor John MacArthur is spineless. They both maintain their positions—but they are respectful of those who hold opposing views.

So it is with New Life Church and Village Seven Presbyterian and Temple Shalom and the Catholic diocese. I am an Armenian charismatic. I am not a five-point Calvinist. I believe firmly that Jesus is the Messiah. I do not accept Rome as the authority for the church. At the same time, I respect reformed theology. I love my Jewish friends. I have great appreciation for Bishop Sheradon, our Roman Catholic bishop here in Colorado Springs, and those who serve with him.

⋆ ⋆ ⋆ ⋆ ⋆

Speaking respectfully and thoughtfully about others can never hurt us.

⋆ ⋆ ⋆ ⋆ ⋆

I have always spoken respectfully about the State of Israel and supported its safety. Because of this, I have been fortunate to form good relationships with the Israeli government and have had opportunity to counsel with Prime Minister Ariel Sharon on a few occasions.

Sometimes we must choose battles to fight, and we must choose wisely. I have different values and theology from many Jews, just as I have different values and theology from the National Council of Churches (NCC). When the NCC released a statement saying that businesses in the Gaza Strip should withdraw—an idea that risked increasing poverty in an already impoverished area—the NAE was forced to issue a very clear and strong rebuttal, because a deliberate political move that increases poverty is contrary to our calling in Scripture and the heart of God. We must be supportive with our speech and actions, but we must also be wise as to where that support is given and to what degree.

JUST DO IT

In Colorado Springs there was a small fundamentalist Bible church that was very exclusive. They would print "King James only—noncharismatic" in their newspaper advertisements. For years they taught that no one could be genuinely born again without using the King James Version and that other Bibles and all other churches were prostitutes of the world.

Then this exclusive congregation found itself in the middle of a battle over zoning that would have put a pornographic bookstore next to their church. They won, but it cost them a fortune in legal fees.

In the midst of their struggle, I tried on several occasions to call the pastor. He was never available. Then one day when I called, I told the secretary we wanted to help with the legal expenses. The pastor called me back within ten minutes. I asked him how much they still owed and told him New Life Church would send his church the amount needed to pay the balance.

He was very pleased.

I have never spoken with this brother about old texts and modern translations, but I have heard that he no longer preaches that the King James Version is the only Bible God can use to speak to people. I have never spoken with this brother about cessationist dispensationalism and its contrast to charismatic theology, but he no longer teaches that people who speak in tongues are demonized. I have never spoken with this brother about the various cultural expressions within the body of Christ, but he no longer teaches that his church's way is the only way to worship.

I think this pastor may have felt as if he didn't have any friends in the Christian community until we made a concrete gesture of friendship. When he realized that other people in the community accepted him, it changed his attitude.

Recently, I was in a restaurant when a man approached me. "You're the pastor of New Life, aren't you?" I nodded. He continued with a big smile, "I just wanted to let you know that I went to your church to see the play 'Heaven's Gates and Hell's Flames.' You have a great church."

, , , , ,

Sometimes we must choose battles to fight, and we must choose wisely.

, , , , ,

Just before he excused himself he mentioned casually which church he attended—the same little church that used to be "King James only" and "noncharismatic."

The Bible says in Ephesians 4:29, "Do not let any unwholesome talk come out of your mouths, but only what is helpful for building others up according to their needs, that it may benefit those who listen." There is no better reason to practice the principles in this chapter than this biblical command. No matter what our own agendas or feelings regarding a situation or another church, we must think first about building others with our words. This takes humility and wisdom, but it can be done, and it always produces more fruit for the kingdom when we obey this command. The Bible also says in Romans 12:20, "If your enemy is hungry, feed him; if he is thirsty, give him something to drink." We are to practice supportive words and actions even when we want to tear down rather than build. There is no better example of this principle than Jesus Himself, who, as He died on a cross at the hands of His own creation, interceded to the Father for all of them.

SPIRITUAL WARFARE

Paul says that strongholds are "arguments" and "pretensions" that work against the knowledge of God and that they need to be pulled down through divine power (2 Cor. 10:4–5). In other words, strongholds are ideas, thoughts, or worldviews people hold that are contrary to God's ways.

Supportive speech and actions negate demonic attempts to build strongholds in us against others. When we say good things about each other and do good things for each other, we are using spiritual weapons. When people are committed to blessing each other, neither the world nor the devil has the power to poison those relationships. Divisiveness, territorialism, bitterness, hatred, and jealousy are unable to gain a foothold. As a result, the Holy Spirit has great opportunity to build a strong coalition in the body of Christ that can make a significant impact on our communities.

››››

No matter what our own agendas or feelings regarding a situation or another church, we must think first about building others with our words.

››››

Spiritual warfare is usually not thought of in these terms. We engage in spiritual warfare while praying, and that is effective. But there are other ways to do spiritual warfare—through our actions and speech.

SEVEN POWER POINTS OF LIFESTYLE WARFARE

ONE SUNDAY MORNING after I taught on spiritual warfare, a pleasant young man came up to me to talk.

"Pastor Haggard," he began, "do you think spiritual warfare can help me overcome my addiction to pornography?"

"Of course," I replied.

"I'm so glad to hear you say that," he answered. "I struggle with pornography. But after I've been online, I rebuke the strongholds of pornography in Jesus' name. That way the demons can't take advantage of me."

He was wrong.

Spiritual warfare is not always just a prayer on your lips. For this brother, spiritual warfare would have been to avoid the adult Web sites and find some believers who would help him stay pure. The act of going to the right place and avoiding the wrong place is as much a part of spiritual warfare as saying a prayer.

LIFESTYLE WARFARE

Spiritual warfare goes beyond the words that we say in prayer. Spiritual warfare also takes place when:

- We tell the truth instead of a lie.
- We choose to stay faithful to our spouses.
- We protect our children.

- We encourage instead of judge.
- We smile instead of frown.
- We treat people with respect.
- We serve instead of control.

I call these actions *lifestyle warfare*. Spiritual warfare starts with verbal prayers, but it doesn't end there. Spiritual warfare occurs not only in our prayer closets but also in the way we demonstrate the character of Christ in our daily living.

The goals of spiritual warfare are to stimulate the activity of the Holy Spirit and hinder the work of Satan. Lifestyle warfare, in these terms, has the same effects as the traditional, prayer-focused versions of spiritual warfare. What happens when you choose Mountain Dew over Budweiser? You open your heart for the ministry of the Holy Spirit and eliminate demonic opportunities. What happens when you spend time building relationships with your children? You open hearts for the ministry of the Holy Spirit and eliminate demonic opportunities. What happens when you honor your boss at work? You open the way for the ministry of the Holy Spirit and eliminate demonic opportunities. Lifestyle warfare provides opportunity for the ministry of the Holy Spirit, blocks satanic opportunity, earns us the right to be heard in the non-Christian community, and makes it hard to go to hell from our cities.

What good would it do if we prayed for people but then treated them with disdain? Instead, we pray for people and also live honorable lives in front of them. Then, they are not only being ministered to by the Holy Spirit in response to our prayers, but they are also seeing the Christian life validated by our actions.

What good would it do if we pray to negate demonic activity among people but then refuse to submit to the delegated authorities in that region? Our prayers might actually be negated by our actions. What good would it do to pray for more manifestations of God's kingdom in the darkest nations of the world and then treat our employees badly or refuse to pay our bills? People won't want more of that kind of kingdom.

Please don't misunderstand me. I believe that communion with

God and confrontation with evil powers in prayer are absolutely essential to prepare any people for the presentation of the gospel. But I also know they are much more effective when accompanied by life-style warfare.

Total spiritual warfare is like using a spear. Our verbal prayers are the tip of the spear, and our lifestyle is the shaft. Throwing the tip of a spear is not very effective. Neither is throwing the shaft. But if you use the spear tip and shaft together, you will have a powerful weapon.

In the next seven chapters, I am going to describe seven power points of lifestyle warfare. As you read and implement them, you will become a more powerful, capable, and competent Christian.

—NINE—

LIVING IN THE TREE OF LIFE

(POWER POINT #1)

I F YOU HAVEN'T read or seen *Les Miserables*, stop reading this book right now and go get the DVD. I have seen the movie and the play, and I appreciate the fact that Victor Hugo's story reveals one of the greatest truths of Scripture. Often, people who strive to be perfectly godly miss the point completely and end up being enemies of God's plan (the Pharisees, Sadducees, Muslim fundamentalists, Christian legalists, etc.), while the imperfect but grateful person who humbly seeks God's grace ends up being an authentic minister.

In *Les Miserables*, a convict named Jean Valjean is released from a French prison after serving nineteen years for stealing a loaf of bread and for subsequent attempts to escape from prison. When Valjean arrives at the town of Digne, no one is willing to give him shelter because he is an ex-convict. In his desperation, Valjean happens to knock on the door of Monseigneur Myriel, the bishop of Digne. Myriel treats Valjean with kindness, but Valjean steals his silverware. When the police arrest Valjean, Myriel covers for him, claiming that the silverware was a gift. The authorities release Valjean, and Myriel makes him promise to become an honest man. Eager to fulfill his promise, Valjean changes his identity and enters the town of Montreuil. Under the assumed name of Madeleine, Valjean invents an ingenious manufacturing process that brings the town prosperity. He eventually becomes the town's mayor.

In keeping with the theme of Scripture, the criminal in this story finds redemption and does a great deal of good. He is the picture of a grateful heart. Also in keeping with well-known scriptural themes, in *Les Miserables* the most "perfect" person is also the worst person—a police officer named Javert who always does the right thing but could not be more wrong. Javert believes in law and order and will stop at nothing to enforce France's harsh criminal laws. He is incapable of compassion or pity, like an animal on the chase. He nurses an especially strong desire to capture Valjean, whose prosperity Javert sees as an affront to justice. Ultimately, Javert contemplates that goodness is more complex than simple obedience to the rules; in the end, he is unable to say with certainty that Valjean deserves to be punished. This ambiguity undermines Javert's beliefs and forces him to choose between hypocrisy and honor.

, , , , ,

Living in the tree of the knowledge of good and evil means making choices based on what is right and what is wrong—which leads to death in us and possibly in those around us.

, , , , ,

This is the exact struggle that happens in every person who wants to be godly. In fact, it is one of the first conflicts portrayed in the Bible. In the Garden of Eden, Adam and Eve had to choose between the tree of life and the tree of the knowledge of good and evil. We all have to choose between these two trees every day.

CHOICES IN THE GARDEN

In the Garden of Eden, Adam and Eve lived in the life of God until the serpent came to Eve and tempted her. She chose the knowledge of good and evil, and her husband did the same (Gen. 2:16–17; 3:1–24). Instead of choosing life, they chose death.

Living in the tree of life means making choices that will lead to more and more life—in our lives and in the lives of those around us. Living in the tree of the knowledge of good and evil means making choices based on what is right and what is wrong—which leads to death in us and possibly in those around us.

As a young man, I could never understand why some devoted Christian people could be so mean. Or why some holy people were so angry. Or why churches could be so correct in their doctrine and be so bitter against others—until I understood the difference between the two trees.

You can read the Bible from the tree-of-life perspective and find redemption, healing, trust, and peace. Or you can read your Bible from the tree-of-the-knowledge-of-good-and-evil perspective and become legalistic and condemn everyone who doesn't agree with you. Unfortunately, some miss the point of their Bibles and use God's Word as a weapon of tyranny.

For example, let's say that you decide to read your Bible every day because that is a good thing to do. After all, the Bible says to hide the Word in your heart. So you read your Bible every day, but you become arrogant about it. Then when you find somebody who doesn't read the Bible every day, you say, "If you were really a good Christian, you would read your Bible every day."

But reading your Bible every day from the tree of life is totally different. You're saying, "I love reading the Bible every chance I get. The life of God flows into me as I read my Bible. It makes me want to pray more, and then I pray more, and it makes me want to read my Bible more. I tell you what, the Bible is the greatest thing I have ever found!"

Then, when someone tells you that he doesn't read his Bible every day, you say, "Brother, you've got to discover this book! It's a wonderful book; it's a life-giving book; it's a liberating book. It tells you how to have a great marriage and how to have a good business and how to treat people and how to forgive people. The Bible is the way to go."

, , , , ,

**Living in the tree of life means making choices
that will lead to more and more life—
in our lives and in the lives of those around us.**

, , , , ,

Living according to the tree of life means you live in a way that brings life to you and others. You do what the Bible says, and you serve other people with joy. You have an attitude of gratefulness because of Jesus' love working in you.

Choosing the tree of knowledge makes you filter everything through a value system of judging what is good and what is evil. Obviously, you cannot find His life in knowing what is good and evil. If you are an expert on what is good, you will judge yourself and others so harshly that you will die. If you are an expert on evil, corruption will creep into your heart and kill you. Knowledge of good and evil always has the same result: death.

That's why Jesus wants us to choose His life.

SAFE TO BE RESCUED

Jesus wants us to have the kinds of churches where He can rescue people. He wants us to be lifeguards, not umpires.

When Jesus was teaching in the temple, the Pharisees brought in a woman who had been caught in adultery. The Pharisees wanted her to sin no more. To them, that meant judging her sin and giving her what she deserved according to the Law—death by stoning. Jesus also wanted her to sin no more. But He offered her life so that she could live in righteousness.

Both Jesus and the Pharisees were trying to accomplish the same thing. But one resulted in death and the other in life.

TRAINING CHILDREN IN THE TREE OF LIFE

Many people who are living in the tree of the knowledge of good and evil believe they are doing the right thing for God. But they can lose sight of the big picture. I see this happen all the time in raising children.

Most Christian parents have a great deal of appreciation for the mercy of God, and they live in the tree of life. But when it comes to raising their children, they change it into a value system based on their knowledge of good and evil. So they raise their children accordingly, and their children resent it—unless the children stumble onto the tree of life themselves. Some do, but not nearly as many as we would like.

I know of a wonderful couple that had two easy-to-raise sons. Then they had a strong-willed daughter and didn't know what to do with her. They tried to keep her in line with their knowledge of good and evil, but she rebelled. It wasn't until she was in a Christian rehabilitation program that the parents realized how they had raised their daughter in the tree of the knowledge of good and evil but had never directed her to the tree of life. Now, they and their daughter have discovered the life of God together.

The Scriptures say, "Train up a child in the way he should go, and when he is old he will not depart from it" (Prov. 22:6, NKJV). "The way he should go" does not refer to our understanding of good and evil. Instead, the way children should go is a lifestyle of seeking life; then they will not depart from it.

BITTERNESS AND FORGIVENESS

When people are angry or bitter and living in unforgiveness, they have slipped into the tree of the knowledge of good and evil. They have passed judgment on a difficult situation and have decided who was good and who was to blame. Technically, they may be right about a particular situation, but being right does not necessarily bring them into life. As a matter of fact, being right is practically irrelevant and sometimes counterproductive if it's poisoning you, making you bitter, or destroying your freedom in prayer. So, you may be right, but you're dead right.

After Adam and Eve ate from the tree of the knowledge of good and evil, the shame and embarrassment caused them to blame one another. Adam said Eve was to blame. Eve said the serpent was to blame. Immediately they displaced their personal responsibility and hid from their best friend, God. That's exactly what happens to us today if we react to circumstances based on the tree of knowledge— we end up blaming others for our failures and hiding from God.

Whenever we start blaming others, we are really declaring their lordship in our lives. When we blame others we are saying, "God, You are not in charge of my life any longer. Eve is, or the serpent is, or my circumstances are, but You are not."

When you say, "Every time I try to pray, I think about George and the thirty thousand dollars he stole from me," you might as well go ahead and say, "George is my lord." You have abdicated authority in your life to someone who has wronged you. You have taken on a victim mentality.

If you are in this kind of situation with anyone or anything, plunge back into the tree of life before the knowledge of good and evil kills you. The tree of life says, "Forgive them. Release them. Trust the Lord." You may still need to take some action, but it must be from a pure heart. If you don't have a pure heart, it would be better to be wronged than to take action. Why? Because forgiveness and trusting the Lord will bring life to you and to those around you.

,,,,,

Whenever we start blaming others, we are really declaring their lordship in our lives.

,,,,,

When you choose the tree of life and refuse to be controlled by the knowledge of good and evil, it disorients demonic strategies. They can't manipulate reactions that come from the tree of life, so they can't develop situations that can control and distract you.

As a matter of fact, the tree of life disempowers human enemies as well. Some people intentionally try to make us angry or bitter. Often, they want us to hate their enemies with them. But when we choose to stay in the tree of life, it keeps us free from ungodly control.

Justice does not demand that we protect the life of God in our hearts. Instead, justice says, "Argue your point. Win over your enemy. Prove that you're right. Win!" Life, though, thrives on mercy and forgiveness. God knew that the knowledge of good and evil would kill us, so we must consciously choose actions that foster life.

As Christians, we have only one enemy, and he is the devil. No human being on earth is our enemy. If we are convinced that somebody is our enemy, we need to love that person, forgive him, pray for him, and be so gentle and kind and loving that Satan can't get his claws into us.

TREE OF LIFE WARFARE

Living in the tree of life is lifestyle warfare. It tears down the kingdom of Satan and promotes the kingdom of God with every decision we make.

Why do we praise God?

Because it stimulates His life in our lives.

Why do we attend church? Why do we treat people with kindness? Why do we forgive? Why do we turn the other cheek? Why do we give tithes and offerings? Why do we care for the poor? Why do we reject offenses?

Because it stimulates His life in us and others.

Why do we avoid hatred? Why do we avoid immorality? Why do we refuse drugs?

Because they promote death in us and those around us.

Remember: in the tree of life, we do the things that bring life to all people, including us.

Finally, let's apply tree-of-life thinking to the advance of the gospel around the world. Think what would happen if we attempted the five primary principles from Section II of this book according to the tree of the knowledge of good and evil. We would get angry at ourselves and other people anytime we didn't do them right. We would be arguing with each other and blaming whoever we felt was "the problem." As a result, the five principles would be much less effective at changing the spiritual climate.

But when we live out the five principles from the tree of life, our hearts don't become dark if mistakes are made. Our motivation is not to execute the principles perfectly. It is simply to bring life to the people around us.

THE NATURAL RESULT: INNOCENCE

The first thing I look for when considering a new staff member is innocence. If a person conveys innocence, I know they understand living in the tree of life.

Jesus addressed the need for an innocent heart when He said, "I tell you the truth, unless you change and become like little children, you will never enter the kingdom of heaven" (Matt. 18:3).

Jesus loved innocence. He seemed to be chuckling when He said, "I praise you, Father, Lord of heaven and earth, because you have hidden these things from the wise and learned, and revealed them to little children. Yes, Father, for this was your good pleasure" (Matt. 11:25–26).

What was the Father's pleasure? To reveal spiritual truths to humble people who had a simple, heartfelt love for Him. I am convinced that this verse explains why some people are so knowledgeable but lack the freedom and power in life to demonstrate genuine Christlikeness.

Childlike innocence is easy to identify. An easy laugh, a quick smile, instant forgiveness, and a wholesome sparkle in the eye all mark those who protect their innocence. It's easy to be friends with innocent people. And it seems as if those who understand innocence easily cultivate long-term relationships, an effective prayer life, and a special anointing in the Holy Spirit.

But negative relationships and the injustices of the world are constantly trying to steal our innocence. They tempt us to be angry, bitter, resentful, greedy, or hateful. Jesus knew that His disciples would have to deal with wickedness, just as we do. So His instruction to them included an admonition to be innocent: "I am sending you out like sheep among wolves. Therefore be as shrewd as snakes and as innocent as doves" (Matt. 10:16).

How are we supposed to appropriate and maintain innocence?

1. *Live in the tree of life, not in the tree of the knowledge of good and evil.* When we make our decisions and evaluations from a tree-of-life perspective, the natural by-product is innocence. As we protect the innocence God so freely gives, the next natural benefit is the free operation of the fruit and the gifts of the Spirit.

2. *Walk in forgiveness.* Every one of us has opportunities to be hurt, disappointed, rejected, or offended every day. If we allow those events to cause us to resent others and think negatively of them, we can no longer serve them effectively or represent the gospel to them. I believe we need to forgive them weekly, and in some cases *daily*, in order for innocence to remain dominant in our lives.

3. *Discern the root of bitterness and reject it at all costs (Heb. 12:15).* People become bitter for a reason, but those reasons are never as terrible as the bitterness that follows. Whether the bitterness is growing in us or in someone we know, we must make sure that it is dealt with immediately. In order to protect my innocence, I never take on someone else's bitterness. To keep from doing this, I won't let people talk to me if they are attempting to cause me to be bitter along with them. I'll pray with them, but if they insist on keeping their bitterness, I'll try to redirect them toward a positive course of action. If that doesn't work, then I'll reconsider the closeness of our relationship until they can forgive.

4. *Let love cover the sins of others.* Love means that we will do what's best for another rather than what's best for us. Many times, in order for us to maintain our lives and the lives of others in the tree of life, we must let love cover over a multitude of sins (1 Pet. 4:8) and intentionally keep no record of wrongs (1 Cor. 13:5). I have found that the best way to do that is to be willing to forget other people's failures or problems, pray about certain situations but never talk to others about them, and simply mind my own business. In

other words, there is an honorable role in acting as if we don't know too much, though there are certainly times when this course of action is not possible. I need to understand that my role is not to cause everyone to fit into my understanding of what is good or evil about them, but rather my role is to keep myself and them growing in the tree of life, thus protecting the innocence of us both.

5. *Practice verbal spiritual warfare.* During times of prayer it is important to commune with God and confront demonic influences. I believe that binding and loosing are an important part of protecting innocence (Matt. 16:19). For example, you may need to bind selfishness, self-pity, greed, inferiority, and arrogance and loose love, concern for others, giving, confidence, and humility. Address demonic influences as quickly as possible, and loose the ministry of the Holy Spirit. That way you will flow in the refreshing that is offered through the life of the Lord Jesus.

The enemy hates it when we live in the tree of life and protect our innocence. His goal is to seduce us into making our decisions based on our knowledge of good and evil, which makes us victims and causes us to blame others. Once we blame others for negative situations, those whom we blame become our lord, and the enemy has accomplished his goal—death. In Christ we do not need to be victimized in any way, nor do we need to victimize anyone else. But should we ever accept victimization—the immediate consequence of being dominated by the sinful nature—the world and demonic influences will begin to shape our lives.

Life is better than knowledge of good and evil.

Innocence is better than victimization.

The ministry of the Holy Spirit is better than the acts of the sinful nature.

There is great power in innocence. According to Proverbs 21:8, "The way of the guilty is devious, but the conduct of the innocent is upright." In innocence we find freedom to pray, socialize with others, and minister to anyone. Innocent people don't need to avoid others, hide anything, or be ashamed or embarrassed. Innocence fosters boldness, life, joy, and inspiration. Innocence is always the natural by-product of an encounter with life.

In order to accomplish our primary purpose, we must choose life and protect our innocence. Then the opportunity exists to make it hard to go to hell from our cities.

—Ten—

Practicing Forgiveness

(Power Point #2)

F ORGIVENESS IS AT the core of who we are as believers. It is foundational to our faith, our message, and our way of life. Christ died for us, reconciling our lives to God through the forgiveness of sins, and all of us enjoy the many blessings that accompany this forgiveness. Freedom, life, grace, peace, strength, and a clean conscience are just a few of the benefits of this wonderful gift. But, interestingly enough, many Christians struggle to walk in this same forgiveness toward others who have wounded or violated them.

For those people, it may be surprising to realize that God's forgiveness is actually "conditional."

Matthew 6:14–15 says plainly, "For if you forgive men when they sin against you, your heavenly Father will also forgive you. But if you do not forgive men their sins, your Father will not forgive your sins." Jesus was teaching a fundamental principle for living out our faith. Forgiveness is the key that unlocks the door to eternal life. But it's not just God's forgiveness of our sins but also our forgiveness of others who have sinned against us.

This principle is highlighted again in Matthew 18:21–35 in the parable of the unmerciful servant. Peter questions Jesus on forgiveness and implies that we might be incredibly forgiving toward others if we forgive them up to seven times. Jesus' response was to give him a seemingly unattainable standard: forgive people seventy times seven times. He then proceeded to tell the story of a man who had a massive debt canceled by his master. This man's life, reputation, and family had been threatened, but after pleading with his master, he was forgiven the entire amount. He immediately went out and found a person who owed him a small amount of money and threatened to throw him and his family in jail until he paid the full amount. This he did even in the face of pleading by the debtor. His master heard about his cruelty, called him to account for his actions, ordered him punished, and called him wicked. Jesus' final words of the story are chilling: "This is how my heavenly Father will treat each of you unless you forgive your brother from your heart."

, , , , ,

Forgiveness has nothing to do with who is right or wrong. Nor does it mean that we condone what that person did. It simply means that we will not let another person's sin ruin our lives.

, , , , ,

The point is that unforgiveness will ruin your life. This man had difficulty grasping the forgiveness that he had received. His monstrous debt had been canceled, but he continued to act as if he was still under the pressure of a tremendous financial burden. He had experienced forgiveness from another, but he did not know how to make forgiveness a way of life.

Why do we hesitate to forgive when we have received such mercy from our heavenly Father? One reason we withhold forgiveness when we are offended is because we are sure that the other person is wrong! But forgiveness has nothing to do with who is right or wrong. Nor does it mean that we condone what that person did. It simply means that we will not let another person's sin ruin our lives. Forgiveness is the natural result of living in the tree of life. It will bring life to us and to the person we forgive. But spending our time contemplating who is right or wrong only leads to death. The person in the wrong is condemned, and the person in the right feels victimized. No one wins.

Another reason we don't easily forgive is because we may think the person who sinned against us is not repentant. It just seems easier to forgive someone who is sincerely sorry for his or her sin. Unfortunately, Jesus makes no provision for forgiveness that is contingent on another person's repentance. Jesus Himself provided forgiveness through His shed blood before we ever responded. He is our model. We have the responsibility to forgive others regardless of their response to us because forgiveness is a protecting force for our lives. Forgiveness saves us from judgment, hatred, resentment, and bitterness. Forgiveness actually prevents someone else's actions from producing hurts, wrong attitudes, or bitterness in us.

BITTERNESS

When we stop forgiving, we open ourselves up to the enemy's schemes. Unforgiveness leads us down the path of anger, malice, jealousy, pride, and a long list of other problems. One of the most destructive of these negative attitudes is bitterness.

The Book of Acts gives us a practical illustration of the effects of bitterness. In Acts 8:9–25, a man called Simon the sorcerer, a cultic magician, offers money to the apostles in order to buy the power of the Holy Spirit. After Peter rebukes Simon, he identifies the man's true spiritual problem: "I see that you are full of bitterness and captive to sin" (v. 23).

These two conditions, bitterness and sin, always go hand in hand. Because of Simon's bitterness, he was unable to understand the spiritual depth of what he saw Peter doing—praying for people to receive the baptism in the Holy Spirit. Everything Simon saw became distorted in his mind. He was unable to grasp eternal events clearly.

The same thing happens today in someone who becomes bitter through failure to forgive. As bitterness makes him captive to sin, a clear perspective of life and spiritual realities becomes impossible. That's why unforgiving people are so relationally destructive. They can't see the big picture of God's purposes in their own lives or the people around them. They are blinded by bitterness.

PHYSICAL ILLNESS

I do not believe, of course, that every problem or sickness is the result of an unforgiving spirit. But people can actually become physically ill because of bitterness and unforgiveness. I know a man in our church who has destroyed his relationships with his family because of a divorce that happened many years ago. The kids in the family have tried again and again to reconcile their relationship with their father, but to no avail. He is aloof and withdrawn. The ex-wife, who is now remarried, has tried to make the relationship cordial and kind, but she has not succeeded. Interestingly, this man has had a continuous series of sicknesses, infirmities, and hospitalizations since the divorce. The doctors can never quite explain what is causing these symptoms, but they do their best and send him back on his way. Knowing this man, I believe it is his inability and unwillingness to forgive those who have wounded him. He lives a stress-filled, bitter, guilt-ridden life. He can't see life clearly. He has few friends, and his body is suffering the effects of his spiritual sickness.

, , , , ,

Unforgiving people are relationally destructive. They can't see the big picture of God's purposes in their own lives or the people around them. They are blinded by bitterness.

, , , , ,

Forgiveness reduces stress. Nursing a grudge can place the same strains—tense muscles, back pain, elevated blood pressure, increased sweating—on your body as a major stressful event. Forgiveness is good for you.

When someone wrongs us, we need to release that person to the Lord and forgive so that we can receive freedom to grow in Christ and fulfill God's plan for our lives. When people finally forgive, they often experience a dramatic healing or receive emotional freedom like never before. It's in our best interests to trust God, forgive others, and let the Lord defend us.

LIFE TO THOSE AROUND US

After we forgive someone for offending us, the door is also open for God's Spirit to work in that person.

An excellent Bible example of this principle is Stephen and his attitude toward those who were stoning him to death. While they were hurling the stones, Stephen said, "Lord, do not hold this sin against them" (Acts 7:60). This forgiving attitude released the grace of God to work in the hearts of the very people committing the offense. One of those people was a man named Saul who desperately needed that grace. As the witnesses laid their clothes at his feet, the seeds of Stephen's forgiveness were planted in the apostle Paul's heart. As history records, God's grace transformed Saul into Paul on the road to Damascus, and after three days of blindness, God opened his eyes to extraordinary forgiveness.

This biblical principle is vitally important for believers to understand. The offended Christian must release the offender to God, or the grace of God won't have the liberty to work in the offender. Trusting Jesus as defender is true faith.

When Pope John Paul II died, one story was told over and over again to encapsulate the character and nature of this great man. We were all reminded once more of his incredible act of forgiveness toward the man who had tried to assassinate him. After Pope John Paul II's recovery, he visited the man in prison, prayed with him, and forgave him for his murderous act. Not only was this a defining moment for the pope's reputation, but it was also a defining moment for this prisoner, resulting in his repentance and conversion. Pope John Paul II's forgiveness had a powerful effect on this man's heart. It opened him up to God's love and mercy.

Several years ago a woman in a nearby church started spreading vicious, untrue rumors about me. The effect of her gossip was far reaching, and it negatively impacted people to whom I was trying to minister. She was sweet and cordial to me in my presence, but when I was absent, she slandered my life, work, and activities.

As I thought about how to confront the situation, I decided that I needed a clean heart first. Each evening I went for a walk and told

God I forgave this woman. Although her stories grew worse and I was deeply offended, I was determined to be clean inside before I confronted her. So I continued my evening declarations of forgiveness.

Then one night God dropped genuine forgiveness into my heart. By His grace I had actually come to love the woman. Now I was no longer emotionally involved with what she said. I was ready to deal with her when God opened the door. To my amazement, once I released her through forgiveness, I didn't have to confront her. God did it for me. I haven't heard one wicked word from her since.

Forgiveness triggers God's intervention! Forgiveness clears the way for God's grace to prevail. Forgiveness releases our control on the situation and affirms our trust in God's ability to come to our defense. When we forgive, we are accepting that Jesus is our defender. He is our protector, so we can forgive!

Jesus is also the best example of a forgiver. When we all turned our backs on Him while He hung on the cross, He opened us to God's grace by saying, "Father, forgive them for they do not know what they are doing" (Luke 23:34).

, , , , ,

Forgiveness releases our control on the situation and affirms our trust in God's ability to come to our defense.

, , , , ,

If we want to open the door for God to influence people in a powerful way, forgiveness is the most effective method. Jesus taught it, Paul practiced it, and experience demonstrates it. Forgive.

Keeping Your Heart Clean

Jesus encourages us not to enter into personal conflict or arguments over temporal issues such as money, houses, clothing, or personal pride. Why? Because our hearts can't handle it. As soon as we enter into personal debate with "enemies," we find that our natural responses to fight, worry, and become bitter take precedence over our spiritual concern to liberate people from bondage. Our perspective moves from the eternal to the temporal, and we risk losing the victory Jesus provides.

Because Jesus understands these natural tendencies, He gives clear instructions about how we are to handle our enemies. He said, "Love your enemies and pray for those who persecute you" (Matt. 5:44). Why did He say this? So our hearts will stay clean. That's why He tells us, "If you are offering your gift at the altar and there remember that your brother has something against you, leave your gift there....First go and be reconciled to your brother; then come and offer your gift" (vv. 23–24). God is most interested in our eternal destinies. His priority is the relationships people have with one another that provide the conduit of ministry. That is why He puts a high value on getting those relationships right. It is more important than sacrifice. It has a higher value than worship. It is more influential than any gift we could give to God.

Jesus also knows the devastation that can occur in the heart of a person in willful conflict with another over temporal things.

> Settle matters quickly with your adversary who is taking you to court. Do it while you are still with him on the way, or he may hand you over to the judge, and the judge may hand you over to the officer, and you may be thrown into prison. I tell you the truth; you will not get out until you have paid the last penny.
>
> —MATTHEW 5:25–26

Notice that the Lord does not promise justice if we are in the right. He doesn't even seem concerned about who is right and who is wrong. Instead He indicates that we should not concentrate on winning or losing, but that the primary goal must be to settle the matter quickly. Jesus knows these conflicts are futile and that they pollute our hearts. If we trust Him and obey His Word concerning our enemies, be assured that He can defend us.

The enemy (Satan) works to produce hatred in the heart of the Christian. Because of his schemes, we must determine never to let any other person ruin our lives by making us hate them. If anyone succeeds at making us hate them, then we have lost our innocence and our life. But when we love our enemies and pray for those who persecute us, we block the plan of the devil and open the door for the ministry of the Holy Spirit in our hearts as well as in the lives of others. Forgiveness ends a quarrel. Forgiveness undermines a fight. Forgiveness undoes the plan of our enemy.

The apostle Paul, quoting from the Book of Proverbs, wrote: "If your enemy is hungry, feed him; if he is thirsty, give him something to drink. In doing this, you will heap burning coals on his head" (Rom. 12:20). Contrary to popular belief, the "burning coals" are a blessing to the person. Fire was an important commodity in Bible times. People transported it by moving coals, sometimes carrying them in a container on their heads. So to heap burning coals on their heads was to give them a valuable and practical gift as an expression of love.

, , , , ,

In reality, forgiveness is the process of giving up your rights to be angry, vengeful, judgmental, or resentful and allowing God to be the righteous Judge in your situation.

, , , , ,

Jesus Himself probably demonstrated this point best. When the whole of humanity became His enemy, He still gave them His best gift (Rom. 5:6–10). God's forgiveness has had a profound impact on our lives because it changes the nature of our relationship with Him. Once we were His enemies, but now, because of love and forgiveness, we've been drawn close. Jesus has made us His friends.

EFFECTIVE PRAYER

The effectiveness of our prayer life is strategically linked to our relationships with others. Jesus told us, "When you stand praying, if you hold anything against anyone, forgive him, so that your Father in heaven may forgive you your sins" (Mark 11:25). People often lose their desire to pray when they are hurt or wounded. Why? Because they instinctively know that their prayers are hindered by either their unwillingness or inability to forgive.

Only one biblical solution exists, and that is to forgive. God's Word clearly teaches that we are not to fight these battles. He is. But in order for Him to be effective, we must make determined efforts to obey His Word. "For we know him who said, 'It is mine to avenge; I will repay,' and again, 'The Lord will judge his people'" (Heb. 10:30).

The same thought is repeated in Romans 12:19: "Do not take revenge, my friends, but leave room for God's wrath, for it is written: 'It is mine to avenge; I will repay,' says the Lord."

When a person becomes a Christian, he loses many of his rights. One of them is the right to hold a grudge. Paul writes forcefully about forfeiting our rights: "I have been crucified with Christ and I no longer live, but Christ lives in me. The life I live in the body, I live by faith in the Son of God, who loved me and gave himself for me" (Gal. 2:20). Paul here reveals a critical secret to successful Christian living—dying to self.

In reality, forgiveness is the process of giving up your rights to be angry, vengeful, judgmental, or resentful and allowing God to be the righteous Judge in your situation. When we forgive, we make room for God's wisdom and intervention in our lives and the lives of those we forgive.

HOW TO FORGIVE

Many people tell me they would like to forgive, but they have been so deeply offended that they can't forgive. In such situations it may become necessary to engage in spiritual warfare against demonic powers that might keep you bound to unforgiveness. (I address this in my book *Simple Prayers for a Powerful Life*.) In these instances you must stand against demonic spirits and attitudes of unforgiveness, bitterness, rage, disappointment, and other influences that keep you miserable. Evil spirits must be cast out, attitudes renewed by God's Word, and the Holy Spirit of God given freedom to work in order to obtain a genuine spiritual victory.

Sometimes when I've become weary and too frustrated with people, I know that I need to take two or three days to go pray and fast in the mountains. I do this because I know that my intensity is misplaced and I've developed a stronghold in my life or allowed a spirit of disappointment to overtake me. I'll spend the entire first day of a three-day fast forgiving all the people that come to my mind. As I pray, the Lord reminds me of people who have hurt me or disappointed me. Even episodes that I've forgotten will come up, and I'll release them to the Lord. I call them out by name and declare my forgiveness, even if they don't know they've wounded me. I need to forgive them and break the power of unforgiveness in my life. The second and third days of my fast are always much more spiritually productive once I settle the issues of forgiveness. My heart opens up; my eyes can see clearly again; my gratitude for God and my love for others become strong.

′ ′ ′ ′ ′

Force yourself to forgive.
Don't wait for it to happen naturally.
It won't happen.

′ ′ ′ ′ ′

As you pray, remember that forgiveness is a process, and you may need to declare your forgiveness every day to the Lord. As you do this over a period of time, God's grace will break through that tough exterior produced by hurt and grant genuine forgiveness in your heart.

Force yourself to forgive. Don't wait for it to happen naturally. It won't happen. You must take control in the name of Jesus. Each time you do this, God will honor your obedience and fill your heart with forgiveness. Greater freedom in your prayer life will result, and the Lord will greatly develop your spiritual potential.

I recommend that you study the following Scripture verses before going through the prayer of forgiveness: Matthew 6:5–15; Luke 6:27–38; 7:36–50; Ephesians 4:31–32.

PRAYER OF FORGIVENESS

Heavenly Father, in the name of the Lord Jesus Christ, I have a confession to make. Instead of loving certain people I have resented them and have unforgiveness in my heart toward them. In obedience to Your Word, I rebuke a spirit of unforgiveness, rebellion, grief, sorrow, hurt, self-centeredness, and pride, and I command all related spirits to loose their grip on my life.

In the name of the Lord Jesus Christ I now forgive... (List all people, living and dead, who have disappointed, hurt, offended, or wounded you in any way. Also list any organizations or groups that have hurt you. Parents, be sure to forgive your children by name if they have hurt you by not fulfilling your expectations of them. Also, forgive them for being ungrateful and so forth.) *I release all these people in the name of the Lord Jesus Christ.*

Lord, I ask You to forgive all of them, too. In addition, I forgive myself for my own sins and shortcomings and ask You to heal my wounded spirit. In Jesus' name, amen.

—Eleven—

Becoming a Servant

(Power Point #3)

I N Jesus' day the Jewish nation lived under the control of a contingent of Romans who exercised ruthless command over the Jewish citizens. Those controllers were under the dominion of fewer people in Rome, and over those people ultimately came one person, Caesar, who had great power and influence.

This type of control system is typical in society—from the playground to the corporate boardroom to government styles such as the Taliban and Hussein's ruthless regime. You could diagram this as shown in the Illustration 8 on page 122.

In this leadership style there are groups of people controlled by a smaller group of people who are controlled by an even smaller group. This ultimately leads to one influential person who has a great deal of power over others—the majority serving the minority.

It was into this power scheme that Jesus' disciples thought they were stepping by following Christ. They found themselves contending for the "greatest" of the positions in Jesus' kingdom, even involving other family members in the grappling. On these occasions Jesus introduced a new set of ideas for leading people and just how to become the "greatest" in His kingdom. He stated, "If anyone wants to be first, he must be the very last, and the servant of all" (Mark 9:35). He went on to contrast His system of leadership with the world's system by saying:

You know that the rulers of the Gentiles lord it over them, and their high officials exercise authority over them. Not so with you. Instead, whoever wants to become great among you must be your servant, and whoever wants to be first must be your slave—just as the Son of Man did not come to be served, but to serve, and to give his life as a ransom for many.

—MATTHEW 20:25–28

Illustration 8

THE WORLD'S VIEW OF LEADERSHIP

Jesus demonstrated these ideas just before His crucifixion while eating with His disciples. In the middle of dinner He grabbed a towel and began to wash the disciples' feet! This task was reserved for the lowest of the servants in each household. Peter resisted, but Jesus told him, "If you want to be a part of My kingdom, this is the way it works" (author's paraphrase). Illustration 9 on page 123 shows Jesus' model: to get to the top you go to the bottom.

Jesus continually frustrated those who wanted Him to climb to the top of the "power and influence" pyramid. His attitude instead was to work His way to the bottom so He could serve the most people.

When Jesus entered Jerusalem, the Jews were convinced that the time had come for Him to overcome the Roman authorities and the corrupt Jewish rulers who had cooperated with the Romans. They ran into the streets shouting, "Hosanna to the Son of David! Blessed is he who comes in the name of the Lord!" (Matt. 21:9). He didn't cooperate in becoming King this way; instead, He suffered the most humiliating death, rose from the dead, and ascended to heaven. His way of becoming our King was to serve us all in death, burial, and resurrection.

Illustration 9

The Biblical View of Leadership

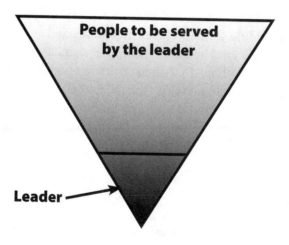

People to be served by the leader

Leader

THE PHILIPPIANS 2 ATTITUDE

Paul understood Jesus' approach to "greatness": to be great in the kingdom of God, you strive to serve the most people. He wrote to the Philippians:

> Do nothing out of selfish ambition or vain conceit, but in humility consider others better than yourselves. Each of you should look not only to your own interests, but also to the interests of others.
>
> Your attitude should be the same as that of Christ Jesus: Who, being in very nature God, did not consider equality with God something to be grasped, but made himself nothing, taking the very nature of a servant, being made in human likeness. And being found in appearance as a man, he humbled himself and became obedient to death—even death on a cross!
>
> —PHILIPPIANS 2:3–8

To understand this in context of Paul's writing, it is important to know that the Philippians had special status within the Roman Empire. Due to their wealth and military history, they had been given privileges, including Roman citizenship status and the "Italic right," which meant their land and citizenship were equal to those living in Rome. Paul taught them that their attitude should reflect Christ's, who, though He was equal with God, sought the status of a servant. To be like Christ, we resist seeking and holding on to status and titles; we just seek and obey. I call this the Philippians 2 attitude. This attitude should permeate all that we do.

- Why do we pray and fast? To gain His power in our lives so we can serve others.

- Why do we read our Bibles? To grow in Him so we know how to serve others.

- Why do we attend church? To worship Him with our fellow believers so we can serve one another and the lost.

- Why do we give tithes and offerings? To honor Him and demonstrate, in a tangible way, our concern for others.

- Why do we live holy lives? To demonstrate that God has changed us and to gain the respect of others so they will allow us to serve them.

- Why do we keep our word? To reflect the nature of the Lord so others will know we are genuine, thus giving us opportunity to serve them.

- Why are we faithful spouses? So our marriages will reflect Christ and His church, opening the door for us to serve others.

- Why do we have budgets? To care for others.

- Why do we need growing churches? To serve others.

The Philippians 2 attitude affects every aspect of life in a positive, powerful way. Jesus teaches us that to find our life we must lose it first. The greatest life is a life lived in servanthood to others.

SERVANTS CHANGE HEARTS

Life takes on an entirely different meaning and is filled with joy and purpose when you look at it from the attitude of serving others. I spoke with a man recently who had started attending New Life Church over the last year. This man had been addicted to drugs for the past forty years of his life but had recently experienced a dramatic change. One of the ministries here that serves the homeless, the addicted, and those in halfway homes had picked this man up, fed him a hot meal, and brought him to church. He was amazed at these people. He was so moved he gave his life to Christ and was delivered from a lifestyle of destruction. His life is now full of joy and vision for the first time ever. His thoughts, once consumed with sin, are now consumed with how he can serve others.

That's a Philippians 2 attitude.

It's using the power and influence that God will give us to help others. To serve.

This idea was preached strongly in the churches in early America. We still see the results today:

- When we want to run for political office, we run to become a *public servant*.

- When we get up to go to church on Sunday morning, we get ready to go to *the service*.

- When we join the military to defend our country, we join *the service*.

- When we paint our police cars, we put on the side, "To protect *and serve*."

Why?

- Because political influence should be used to serve others.

- Because church authority is for the purpose of making the lives of those who attend more godly.

- Because military might is to be used to help people who can't help themselves.

- Because police power in the community is meant to protect citizens and maintain peace.

When the churches of Colorado Springs were participating in the Christmas gospel ad campaign, we got a phone call from a blind woman whose seeing-eye dog had just died. She told the phone counselor, "I don't need to get saved as much as I need a new dog."

We found out what kind of dog she needed, went out and bought one, and delivered it to her the next week. I believe that is what Jesus would have done. Making sure that woman received a new dog was the greatest possible sermon she could have ever received. She didn't pray with us to receive Christ immediately, but her heart opened as she experienced people taking care of her in Jesus' name.

The Salvation Army, Compassion International, and every local church whose members take food to a grieving family or provide a ride to an elderly person or mow the grass for someone who can't do it demonstrate the mind of Christ—the Philippians 2 attitude.

In the twenty-year history of New Life Church, we have had only one fight. It wasn't over the design of a building, the leadership of a class, or a budget question. It was between two women who were fighting over the same vacuum cleaner. They both wanted to serve the church on that Monday morning. I went out and bought another vacuum so they could both serve.

Harmony is unusual because the world trains us to try to control, manipulate, protect our territory, and fight for the top. But when we choose to serve, we confuse demonic schemes because we become unpredictable.

Satan loves to lie to people and say that Christians are no better than anyone else. He capitalizes on the failures of high-profile Christians. But his lies sound hollow when nonbelievers find themselves being served by Christians with no ulterior motives—just a desire to serve.

′ ′ ′ ′ ′

Harmony is unusual because the world trains us to try to control, manipulate, protect our territory, and fight for the top. But when we choose to serve, we confuse demonic schemes because we become unpredictable.

′ ′ ′ ′ ′

This attitude is obvious when you are working to fulfill God's calling on our generation to advance the cause of the Great Commission. What attitude should we have as we do this? One of service to all people. A humble spirit from a servant's attitude causes others to have an open heart toward you. If your attitude reflects your desire to bless them and cause them to be successful with no ulterior motives or sinful manipulation in mind, people will welcome you and open their hearts to you. We become more effective when we work toward the bottom instead of the top.

—Twelve—

Showing Respect

(Power Point #4)

WHETHER WE ARE talking about individuals or churches in our communities, the greatest thing we can do to open the door for ministry is to show respect for others. Recently, I had an experience in my role as the president of the NAE that drove this point home for me. When Senator Arlen Specter was being considered to head up the Senate Judiciary Committee, several Christian leaders were actively voicing their strong disagreement with some of his political views, namely the fact that he's strongly pro-choice. There was concern because we were all convinced that President Bush was going to appoint some judges to the Supreme Court who would be open to considering whether or not a fetus was a human being. Democratic senators had been very clear that they didn't want anyone on the Supreme Court who would even consider the possibility that a fetus might be human, because that contemplation could modify *Roe v. Wade*.

In the midst of this struggle, Senator Specter had expressed views that were interpreted as support for the Democratic view. In response, the evangelical media machine was in full swing to question whether Senator Specter should, in fact, be the chair of the Senate Judiciary Committee—a legitimate concern, no doubt. Parachurch media leaders started using radio, television, e-mail, and snail-mail campaigns, threatening to use political force to deny him the seat if he didn't line up with their views on the issues. Republican leadership went quiet in the heat of the dilemma. The pressure was on.

One of my trips to Washington DC during this time included an appointment with Senator Specter. We had never met, but our staffs had been in communication and had developed a relationship. Even though it was our first meeting, he was cordial and engaging. Before we went into his private office, we found common ground, common values, and some common interests. There was no tension. After we were inside I introduced myself on behalf of the NAE and told him that I was fully aware of the consternation that was associated with the potential of him becoming the chair of the Senate Judiciary Committee. I told him that the 30 million people in the NAE respect the traditions of the Senate, which would place him in the chair, and that I was there to answer any questions he might have about evangelicalism, evangelicals, and how we work.

He wanted to talk. He seemed almost stunned by my words, as if he were expecting me to be antagonistic and argumentative. He was immediately warm and wanted to skip small talk to get to substance. We were scheduled to meet for thirty minutes, but he asked that we stay for an hour until he had to leave to vote. When they called for him to leave, he asked that we stay until after the vote so we could talk some more. When we were done, he expressed an interest in meeting together again. As we left, one of his close associates thanked us profusely and said that we had just been involved with the best meeting he had ever seen in the senator's office.

The next day, the gridlock ended.

I am fully aware that there were many powers and personalities at play in this series of events, and I am 100 percent certain that my meeting did not solve the problem. However, I had a concern—if Senator Specter did receive the chairmanship position for the Senate Judiciary Committee, I didn't want him hostile to evangelical Christians. I knew that he needed additional evangelical representation so that we would have a relationship if, in fact, he received the position, which he did.

The point of this story is not the politics of evangelicalism, but rather the importance of respect. I entered this senator's office with a respect for his position, and it paid off. I now feel that I can have honest, open conversations with him—he respects me and I respect him.

Our staffs can communicate with openness and honesty in an atmosphere of friendship. Had I entered his office with a different mindset, we would have a different kind of relationship today.

People believe what they believe for a reason. I don't believe in a theocracy, and I do embrace the pluralistic nature of our system. I also believe that people respecting one another is vital to communication and getting work done.

An opposite illustration I could give to this point is the way the Bush administration responded to NAE concerns in contrast to the John Kerry campaign during the 2004 election. President Bush had members of his White House staff communicate regularly with evangelical leaders to ensure that they were addressing our areas of interest. Since the NAE is bipartisan and has had to work with both Democratic and Republican administrations through the years, we tried to communicate with the Kerry campaign. We received no returned calls, no notes, no invitations to meetings. Nothing. And, interestingly, since the vote was so close, a little respect from the Kerry campaign toward evangelicals might have changed some things.

, , , , ,

The point of this story is not the politics of evangelicalism, but rather the importance of respect. I entered this senator's office with a respect for his position, and it paid off.

, , , , ,

We must respect one another first and foremost because each of us is created by God in His image. Second, we often must respect others simply because of the position they hold, not necessarily because they are or are not respectable.

I recall a Christian in town who decided that he wanted to start a church in his home after New Life Church had been functioning for about a year. He didn't consult his neighbors or embrace a respectful attitude toward those in authority. Soon the neighbors started complaining about traffic on their street during this brother's Sunday service. Instead of respecting them, he fought his neighbors, fought the city, and ended up in several legal battles trying to defend his church.

By the time the struggle was over, he left the city in the middle of the night, angry at other churches, his own parishioners, and the city. This brother sincerely thought he was fighting for righteousness, but he didn't help the secular community at all in its understanding of the gospel. Plus, he actually made it more difficult for the kingdom of God to expand. If this incident had happened before we started New Life Church in my home, it would probably have caused my neighbors to be excessively cautious, and they would never have let me do it.

Consideration of others goes a long way. I don't believe that we could ever underestimate the power of respect. But while saying that, I recognize that it's not always easy to be respectful—especially in major conflicts.

David's refusal to disrespect King Saul, even though Saul was trying to kill David, is a powerful picture for all of us. Further, Jesus demonstrated respect for the Roman government by paying His taxes, and Paul apologized for not showing respect to the high priest. (See Acts 23:3–5.)

Even in the most difficult personal struggles, being respectful toward others helps keep you and the others involved in the conflict living in the tree of life. Ephesians 5:21 says to "submit to one another out of reverence for Christ." The Bible commands us to be considerate and respectful of others.

Sometimes members of our churches or our churches themselves become involved in litigation as the result of some type of wrongdoing. When we enter the court from a heart's desire to serve our community, the outcome can possibly be beneficial, although I would rarely recommend solving conflicts in court. For certain, if we want to sue to demonstrate our ability to win over someone else or another organization, we would not be reflecting a godly lifestyle.

Prayers prayed during conflicts between people will be hampered if the primary people involved become disrespectful. But when the people involved respect each other, it becomes a great weapon of spiritual warfare. It negates the enemy's opportunity to portray Christians negatively, and it facilitates the ministry of the Holy Spirit.

RESPECTING AUTHORITY = BLESSING

Respect denies the enemy a foothold and fosters the types of relationships that can actually gain ground for the kingdom of God. Therefore, respect is spiritual warfare. Second Corinthians 10:4 says, "The weapons we fight with are not the weapons of the world. On the contrary, they have divine power to demolish strongholds."

I believe we are to respect specific authorities God has delegated in four areas:

1. Family
2. Workplace
3. Government
4. Church

I believe that too often our actions negate our words and our prayers and hurt our ability to touch our cities. We believe that the most important thing we do as Christians is to have good church services. But if we don't understand the significance of issues like the power of respect, people won't care about our church services. They will believe that we are hypocrites unless we live a respectful lifestyle.

FAMILY DYNAMICS

Our ability to foster healthy relationships within our families is a direct indicator of our relationship with the Lord. First Timothy 3:4–5 connects the qualifications for eldership to the attitudes and behaviors of our children, and in 1 Timothy 5:8, Paul writes, "If anyone does not provide for his relatives, and especially for his immediate family, he has denied the faith and is worse than an unbeliever."

It is in the home that we learn to maintain long-term relationships, which is God's desire for His body. Learning to be respectful of others really starts at home with children respecting their parents and parents respecting their children. The disciplines necessary to maintain a healthy family are many of the same required to build integrity within the body of Christ.

WORKPLACE ETHICS

God has also placed most of us in a position where we must submit to authorities within the workplace. First Timothy 6:1–2 speaks about the employee-employer relationship. My paraphrase of this text allows for application in today's culture: "Anyone who works for someone else for their living should consider their supervisors worthy of full respect, so that God's name and our teaching may not be slandered."

Here the Bible directly connects respect for our "bosses" with evangelism. In other words, the Bible indicates that the lifestyles of those who call themselves Christians determine the validity of the message in the minds of their co-workers, associates, and authorities. If you are honest, hard working, and respectful in your place of employment, when the door opens for you to share your faith, it will be received with trust.

GOVERNMENT VALIDITY

In 1 Timothy 2:1–4, the Bible is very clear regarding our responsibility to pray for those in authority over us. In doing so, God will grant "peaceful and quiet lives in all godliness and holiness" (v. 2). In Romans 13:2, Paul equates our attitude toward governing authorities with our attitude toward God: "Consequently, he who rebels against the authority is rebelling against what God has instituted, and those who do so will bring judgment on themselves."

I am leaving in two weeks for a small meeting with Prime Minister Sharon of Israel. When his office called, they said they would meet me at the airport, have a military helicopter give me an overview of the nation, and then take me with several others to talk with the prime minister. Why? Because evangelical leaders are putting pressure on Israel as they are planning to turn land over to the Palestinians. As a result, they want to talk with me to find out what the people in the NAE network of churches think. In other words, they have heard from those who shout; now they want to hear from another whether the shouters are right or not.

LOCAL CHURCH RELATIONSHIPS

I believe relationships in a church are like relationships in a family—you need to build them on respect and plan for them to last. One of the great failures of the modern American church culture is the way we encourage pastors to relocate from church to church every few years. I understand that there are some benefits, but the costs are much higher.

, , , , ,

Churches that foster relationships as a priority over systems, policies, and procedures reap the rewards of a church that passes its legacy on from one generation to the next.

, , , , ,

Our local churches exist for specific purposes, and those purposes hinge on the integrity of healthy, long-term relationships. When we move our pastors often, we deny them the opportunity to learn through lifelong relationships. And both the church and the pastor learn the skills of short-term, superficial relationships—skills that are actually counterproductive.

In a church, it is hoped that as a family raises children, they will know the same people for decades. In this environment, we learn that loose speech, undisciplined behavior, and a haughty attitude will destroy relationships. Churches that foster relationships as a priority over systems, policies, and procedures reap the rewards of a church that passes its legacy on from one generation to the next. When respect is practiced, long-term relationships become natural, and the church community easily prospers.

EARN THE RIGHT TO BE HEARD

Two men from the Middle East operate a local Oriental carpet store here in Colorado Springs. They are both Islamic. Several years ago my wife and I went in to purchase some carpets, and these men and

I became friends. After a long conversation they discovered that I was a "priest." Because of the decency of our conversation, they immediately started asking me extensive questions about God. They were very interested.

Now our friendship is several years old. Every time I am near their store I stop by, and we have wonderful conversations. I am confident that these men have developed great respect for both the gospel and Christians. I may lead them to Christ one day and baptize them, but even if I don't, I'll always respect them.

, , , , ,

If we want to be a church that is respected in our community, we must earn the respect of families, employers and employees, city government, and other churches by demonstrating our respect for them.

, , , , ,

I believe that people are the way they are for a reason and that my role as a Christian is to treat them with respect. I tell myself to treat people as I would want to be treated. Everyone is important, and as people are treated with dignity, their hearts become open to the message of our lives.

There are many church leaders who feel that Christians have been mistreated or misunderstood by the news media. I wonder if part of the reason for that is the lack of respect that we show toward journalists and reporters. If we approach them disrespectfully, is it any surprise that their view of the church might be "biased"? I believe that in part, it is the role of the news media to hold the church accountable. If we will treat them respectfully, I think that we can expect the same in return. We must earn the right to be heard. If we want to be a church that is respected in our community, we must earn the respect of families, employers and employees, city government, and other churches by demonstrating our respect for them.

PRAY FOR THOSE IN AUTHORITY OVER YOU, THEN TRUST THEM

Respect is something that we owe every person as one created in God's image, and in some cases as one who has been placed in a position of authority for whatever reason. I encourage you to make a list of those in authority over you in each of the four areas outlined earlier and pray for those people regularly. In addition, make a list of those under your authority that you are responsible to protect. Pray for them regularly, acting as a faithful prayer shield.

Then start seeing everyone you deal with from the perspective of respect. Even if the situation seems negative, treat people respectfully. With that, the five primary principles will have greater effectiveness in your city.

—Thirteen—

Cultivating Character

(Power Point #5)

Integrity validates our message. Our actions demonstrate whether what we say is true or not. Because our message is Christ's message to the world, that integrity is vitally important. I am convinced that the gospel would have reached everyone in the world centuries ago if it were not for the conflicting messages Christians have sent with actions that did not line up with words.

We have all seen the gospel message maligned because of the actions of someone who claimed to be a Christian. Many who have rejected the gospel don't actually have a problem with the gospel but with the character of the individuals proclaiming it.

The successful accomplishment of our primary purpose rests only in part on our methods of proclaiming the gospel or in our prayer lives. The foundation of fulfilling our purpose is earning the right to be heard because of our personal character.

I preach several times a year at New Life Church about the kind of message we send to nonbelievers through our character. Paul told the Thessalonians, "Make it your ambition to lead a quiet life, to mind your own business and to work with your hands, just as we told you, so that your daily life may win the respect of outsiders and so that you will not be dependent on anybody" (1 Thess. 4:11–12). Paul puts it in very practical terms here: If nonbelievers don't respect you, they are not going to listen to you. And you earn respect through the character you live out every day.

A friend of mine works at a company where there are very few Christians. The one Christian in her department is a man whose work habits are exceptional. He is respectful and pleasant. He is never pushy or arrogant, but helpful and nice. Because of his character he has earned the right to be heard, and through this he has opened the door for the expansion of the kingdom.

> > > > >

Our character can be a deciding factor in somebody else's salvation.

> > > > >

If we pay our bills on time, leave generous tips for waitresses, serve our families faithfully, support our churches, and forgive grudges, others will be more open to us. Think of it this way: our character can be a deciding factor in somebody else's salvation.

The Bible ties character and spiritual warfare together in Ephesians 6, where Paul describes successful spiritual warfare by the wearing of the armor of God. Each piece of the armor points to personal character.

THE BELT OF TRUTH

Telling the truth and wearing a belt do the same thing: they keep things in the right place.

When wearing the belt of truth, our public and private lives validate one another. Probably the easiest way to put on the belt of truth is to live by this motto: "There is no such thing as a secret."

If you want to keep something secret, don't tell it. If you want to do something you don't want certain people to ever know, don't do it. As soon as we believe that we can think, say, or do secret things, there is a greater opportunity for the enemy to persuade us to violate God's Word. After all, the newspaper's best headlines are accounts of people doing things they thought would remain a secret.

When David met with Bathsheba "secretly" and had her husband killed "secretly," he never dreamed those secrets would be discussed openly for thousands of years. When Judas developed a "secret" code to identify Jesus with a kiss, he never thought that code would become the most notable event of his life.

Joseph Stalin, Adolf Hitler, and Pol Pot most likely thought their great public achievements would earn them places in history as great leaders. Instead their "secret" activities are what they are remembered for—the murders of millions of their own citizens.

One more thing about the belt of truth: it is not an exhortation to say everything we know. The Bible exhorts us to use wisdom and discretion in our speech, so it would be foolish to say anything and everything that goes through a person's mind. Our words are to be honest but wise.

Remember: live your life as if there is no such thing as a secret.

THE BREASTPLATE OF RIGHTEOUSNESS

Several years ago a pastor friend of mine had to inform three children that their father had decided to divorce their mother and had left with another woman. When the children heard the heartbreaking news, they became so upset that they were physically sick to their stomachs and vomited. Why? Because the father had removed his breastplate of righteousness. It made his own heart vulnerable to deception and, at the same time, caused the hearts of those who trusted and loved him to become vulnerable.

The purpose of a breastplate is to protect a person's life-giving organs from damage in the midst of war. War? Yes, conflict is guaranteed, but so is victory if we will fight. If we refuse to fight, we will lose. If we fight and keep our breastplate in place, we win. Righteousness protects the hearts of our friends and relatives from the wounds that would be caused by our unrighteousness. Righteousness makes long-term, healthy relationships possible. Righteousness makes us invincible. Righteousness makes us victorious. Righteousness ushers us into the destiny that God has for us. Righteousness is the key to God's prosperity in our lives. It makes our lives impenetrable to accusation, condemnation, and shame. Righteousness surrounds us like steel.

When we remove the breastplate of righteousness, we not only expose our core to destruction, but we also expose all of those under our authority and within our sphere of influence to some degree of destruction.

None of us lives an independent life. Our decisions affect others. So as a husband, if you maintain the breastplate of righteousness, your whole family is protected, stable, and secure. But if you take off the breastplate by sinning, your whole family is violated and becomes more insecure. The same is true for other members of the family.

If you are a business owner and maintain the breastplate of righteousness, your employees and customers will all benefit from your integrity. They will prosper and be secure in their jobs and in the services and products that you provide. If, however, you become selfish and corrupt, then your employees, their families, and your customers will all suffer because of your sinfulness.

If you are in church leadership and lead a righteous life, there will be a sense of security and trust within your sphere of influence. If, however, you remove the breastplate of righteousness, those within the influence of your ministry will become discouraged, and many will reject you. And as a result, some will reject the Lord.

And for those of you in public service, when a public servant is a person of integrity, it brings security to the people. If, however, lies, deceit, and corruption enter into your public service, the citizens will pay.

The blessings that come from righteousness positively impact everyone within our sphere of influence, and the cost of sin negatively impacts them as well.

Put your breastplate on. If you are sinning, stop it right now.

Souls worldwide are hanging in the balance of our integrity. Jesus promised that it would be better to be thrown into the sea with a millstone tied around your neck than to cause another person to stumble. I'm confident that many, many self-proclaimed Christians are candidates for the millstone because of the way they have treated others directly or the way they allowed unrighteousness to enter their lives, thus ruining their testimonies.

The impact of unrighteousness is devastating. Once people are violated by a lack of integrity, they have to wrestle with unforgiveness, bitterness, or anger. Living a righteous life not only keeps our own conscience clean but also protects all of our loved ones for generations to come. The blessings of righteousness or the consequences of violation extend for generations. I have preached a sermon entitled, "So, How Much Is Your Sin Going to Cost Me?" When I am tempted to sin, I stop and think about what my actions will cost others. Very seldom do we think like this in the midst of temptation.

, , , , ,

When we remove the breastplate of righteousness, we not only expose our core to destruction, but we also expose all of those under our authority and within our sphere of influence to some degree of destruction.

, , , , ,

If our relationships are not rooted in righteousness, we, in effect, invalidate our own prayers. Our prayers and our lifestyle must go hand in hand. Why? Because both are spiritual warfare; both hinder demonic activity and increase the Holy Spirit's activity in our lives.

One time I got a call from a woman who was excited to tell me that she had led her neighbors to the Lord and that they would all come to church together on Sunday. When Sunday came, she was there alone. She told me that on Friday night she and her neighbors had celebrated their newfound salvation, and they had enjoyed some drinks together. By the end of the night, everyone had become drunk, and the woman had slept with the husband. The family was angry with her and wouldn't have anything to do with God, the church, or her. Amazingly, she seemed not to understand what had gone wrong.

This is indeed an extreme example, but this happens in less dramatic ways all of the time. In this case, though, her lack of righteousness contradicted her witness so strongly that any positive decisions made by her neighbors were negated. She potentially did more harm than good. That makes me think of an old saying: "Sin will take you farther than you want to go, keep you longer than you want to stay, and cost you more than you can afford to pay."

Remember: live a lifestyle that protects people's hearts.

FEET FITTED WITH THE READINESS THAT COMES FROM THE GOSPEL OF PEACE

This piece of armor is simple. We need to go to the places our purpose in Christ demands us to go. Our "feet" must be Spirit-dominated and obedient to God's Word, free to go where the gospel asks us to go.

Where we choose to go or not go is powerful spiritual warfare. When we attend church, a Bible study, or some other wholesome activity we are strengthened in godliness and, just by our presence, strengthen others. Prayer walking, taking a prayer journey, visiting someplace nice with your family, or enjoying a Little League baseball game with your child increases the Holy Spirit's opportunity for ministry. God likes it when we stay in wholesome, holy, life-giving places.

Conversely, if someone visits a prostitute, an adult bookstore, a bar, or a meeting promoting anti-Christian attitudes, that person gives the devil a foothold in his or her personal life and, simply by being there, encourages others in sinful activities. Likewise, when we neglect the maintenance of our homes and avoid family and church activities, we are in effect hampering the Lord's work in our hearts and the hearts of others.

, , , , ,

The places we choose to go and the places we avoid have direct spiritual significance. Remember, our lifestyles are a form of spiritual warfare.

, , , , ,

Several years ago, a good friend by the name of Britt Hancock and I took three days to pray and fast in downtown Colorado Springs. During that time we walked through the downtown area on prayer walks—taking special time to pray over government buildings, churches, adult bookstores, and bars.

One time while prayer walking we noticed a car with a Christian bumper sticker in an adult bookstore parking lot. I left a note on the car offering assistance to its driver if he would like to call. We waited discreetly for a few minutes to see how the note would be received.

A young man who appeared to be a college student came out of the bookstore and glanced around apprehensively, obviously feeling guilty. He looked embarrassed as he read the note on his car; then he drove away quickly.

He was probably a struggling Christian. He apparently didn't like what he was doing. But by being in the wrong place he was feeding the wrong spirits. His "feet" were not Spirit-led.

I have learned that after men like this sin, they go through extended times of guilt and remorse. They repent fervently and then, sometime later, repeat their sin.

This young man would have accomplished his goal if he had prayed with his actions as well as his words. He should have confessed his struggle to an older, stronger brother and visited a place other than the bookstore. Avoiding the bookstore would have been a more powerful act than an extended time of prayer before or after.

The places we choose to go and the places we avoid have direct spiritual significance. Remember, our lifestyles are a form of spiritual warfare. Sometimes, by our physical presence we can possess places for the kingdom of God; other times we should avoid certain places at all costs. The lifestyle warfare principle is important for all Christians to understand.

Remember: let your calling in Christ determine where you go and where you don't.

THE SHIELD OF FAITH

First John 5:4 says, "For everyone born of God overcomes the world. This is the victory that has overcome the world, even our faith." Every one of our troubles seeks to separate us from the love of Christ. Instead, use them as stepping-stones to victory. Notice in this verse that victory and faith are linked together. Every time you win, you are promoted.

First Corinthians 10:13 says, "No temptation has seized you except what is common to man. And God is faithful; he will not let you be tempted beyond what you can bear. But when you are tempted, he will also provide a way out so that you can stand up under it." Here we have it—there is no battle that is beyond you. God is aware and

He knows your capacity; as 1 John 5:4 reminds us, the shield of faith grants our victory. We need never fail.

During times of prayer and fasting, the Holy Spirit will plant His vision for our lives, our families, and our cities in our hearts. He will show you how much He loves the world. So when you are carrying the shield of faith, it means that you are walking with such confidence in God's vision for yourself that the fiery darts of the enemy don't even arrest your attention.

There have been times when I have received phone calls late on a Saturday night by people threatening to kill me the next morning during church. I simply unplug the phone, roll over, and go back to sleep. When I observe intensive spiritual struggles within our congregation, I just keep praying, preaching the Word, and loving them—just as I normally do—and we stay steady in the midst of the storm. Why?

Because we are born to win. I am convinced that as we walk in faith, we learn that all life's problems have solutions. There are as many victories as there are problems, and we can experience constant victories in all life situations by applying God's Word. God does not intend for us to be up and down, but up all the time. You can always be victorious in Him.

One Sunday morning a member of our maintenance team arrived at the church early and saw evidence that witchcraft incantations had been performed directly outside our front door during the night. He knew my policy on that, so he prayed quietly, cleaned up the mess, and didn't tell me until Wednesday. We prayed and talked, went to lunch, kept serving people, and never told the congregation about it. Why? Because it's a distraction. We didn't need to make a big deal out of it because we know where we're headed.

We are born winners. We are victors. In Christ, we are above defeat and failure. We are in a war that must be won, and we will engage in battles, but we know we will win.

During one of my out-of-town trips one week, my wife, Gayle, received numerous threatening phone calls from a local warlock. The last one she received woke her from a deep sleep right at midnight. It involved a lengthy rhyming incantation that ended with, "Tell all of this to Ted." Still somewhat groggy, all she could think of to reply was,

"Is that all?" The caller slammed down the phone, and she went back to sleep. That was the last time we heard from him.

, , , , ,

There are as many victories as there are problems, and we can experience constant victories in all life situations by applying God's Word.

, , , , ,

The shield of faith frustrates our spiritual enemies because we appear to be apathetic toward them; we give them no respect. In reality we are concerned about them and their spiritual influence, but when they take shots at us, we just raise our shield of faith. (By the way, Satan's most effective "darts" are not necessarily occult intimidation. They can be burnout, sin, wasting time, focusing on differences in the church, sexual temptation, and so on.)

We fight the good fight of faith by diligently, consistently, and faithfully fixing our eyes on His mark and pursuing it for the sake of the lost around the world. How do we war? We obey God's Word. Is that hard to do? No, it's easy. You want a hard life? Live in disobedience. You want a blessed, peaceful, powerful, abundant life? Slip into the ease of obedience as you walk in faith. Then no weapon of the enemy is effective against you, and you have won with God's shield of faith.

Remember: being consumed with His vision leaves no time for distraction.

THE HELMET OF SALVATION

Thoughts precede words, and words precede actions. If a person violates scriptural principles in his thought life, soon his actions will reflect it.

Wearing the helmet of salvation is disciplining our thoughts according to biblical standards. We submit our values and opinions to God's Word and allow His transformation to protect us from the schemes of the enemy.

That's why good books are better than bad books and good movies better than bad movies. That's also why meditation on the Scriptures is life changing. The helmet of salvation—thinking thoughts "saved" people ought to think—enhances the Holy Spirit's opportunities to use us and thwarts the enemy's schemes. It's a lifestyle of warfare.

Paul wrote to the church in Philippi, "Finally, brothers, whatever is true, whatever is noble, whatever is right, whatever is pure, whatever is lovely, whatever is admirable—if anything is excellent or praiseworthy—think about such things" (Phil. 4:8).

In his letter to the Romans, he again teaches the importance of thinking according to God's plan: "Do not conform any longer to the pattern of this world, but be transformed by the renewing of your mind. Then you will be able to test and approve what God's will is— his good, pleasing and perfect will" (Rom. 12:2).

So to put on the helmet of salvation, we learn the Word of God and think according to His plan. In Romans 8:5–7 Paul writes:

> Those who live according to the sinful nature have their minds set on what that nature desires; but those who live in accordance with the Spirit have their minds set on what the Spirit desires. The mind of sinful man is death, but the mind controlled by the Spirit is life and peace; the sinful mind is hostile to God. It does not submit to God's law, nor can it do so.

But how do we start? By applying the blood of Christ to our minds to make powerless the thoughts that can easily cause us to be slaves to sin. Hebrews 9:14 explains the vital work of the blood of Christ in our minds by saying, "How much more, then, will the blood of Christ, who through the eternal Spirit offered himself unblemished to God, cleanse our consciences from acts that lead to death, so that we may serve the living God!"

These passages demonstrate clearly that our success is determined by God's work in our minds, changing the things we think about. If we focus on the obstacles before us, then we will allow those obstacles to dominate our prayers and actions, which will result in our cities remaining in darkness.

Virtually every day when I wake up, I read a portion of Scripture. I take a portion and try to memorize it, and then, when I pray, I pray through the ideas embedded within the scripture that I'm trying to memorize. It comes alive. I'm convinced that if we would meditate upon God's Word, think about it, say it, quote it, refer to it, then we begin to think the way He thinks. I think it's invaluable to memorize a few longer portions of Scripture. Why? For several reasons, but the primary one is that by memorizing large portions of Scripture, we begin to think the way God thinks. And when we think the way He thinks, then we say the things He says and do the things He does. It's worth it.

, , , , ,

Our success is determined by God's work in our minds, changing the things we think about.

, , , , ,

Rearrange your morning schedule so you have time to think, meditate, and memorize, thus putting on a way of thinking that guarantees you the full benefits of the salvation that Christ has freely given you.

Every day we make a choice. We can focus on obstacles or we can pray, study the Word, and put on the helmet of salvation, understanding that God has a plan that needs to be thought about, dreamed about, and considered. In that atmosphere, the Holy Spirit will do the miracles necessary to use us to strengthen our local church and reach out to our neighborhoods, cities, and nations. If we deny the enemy his ground in our thoughts, we win.

Remember: think His thoughts.

THE SWORD OF THE SPIRIT (THE WORD OF GOD)

Jesus set the example of how we should live. Each time the devil tempted Him in the wilderness, Jesus replied by saying "It is written," and then He began to quote Scripture.

If we don't know the Word of God, any demonic or worldly idea may seem reasonable. It is, in fact, the Word of God that keeps mankind from believing he is his own god. If our own opinions, thoughts, or conclusions are our highest authority, we are in serious trouble because we are capable of horrendous thoughts and, therefore, horrendous actions.

God's Word gives us a standard for genuine character. The Word terrifies every demonic stronghold because it develops in all Christians the ability to wage continuous lifestyle warfare with authority and confidence. Secularism crumbles at the Word of God.

We have two interdependent sources of discovering the Word of God—a personal relationship with Jesus Christ, the living Word of God, and the Bible, the written Word of God. (See Hebrews 4:12; John 1:1–2.) Both encourage growth in the other.

From the Bible we discover God's great vision for us, our families, our cities, our nation, and our world. Through relationship with Jesus and communication with His Spirit, we learn tangible methods of negating the world's power and thwarting demonic schemes. These two dynamic forces communicate God's will and methods. When used appropriately, they are always successful.

The information in the Bible is alive. It speaks directly into our situations and gives specific guidance. It teaches us how to keep the snares of the enemy and the failures of our own pasts from entangling us.

That's why we pray the Word of God, sing the Word of God, speak the Word of God, meditate upon the Word of God, and long to be saturated with the Word of God. It is the sword that transforms us from pacifists to activists, from isolated thinkers into city changers, from people pleasers into persuasive promoters of His kingdom.

When Paul was speaking to young Timothy about the importance of God's Word, he said, "All Scripture is God-breathed and is useful for teaching, rebuking, correcting and training in righteousness, so that the man of God may be thoroughly equipped for every good work" (2 Tim. 3:16–17).

If you will think about the benefits listed here from the Scriptures, it will motivate you to dwell in the Scriptures daily. But there is a more subtle idea that stands out to me. Notice that the Bible says, "All Scripture is God-breathed." No doubt, God breathed the ideas of the Scriptures into the heart of the Bible authors, and that's what became our Bible today. But I think there is a contemporary application.

I believe that when we pray about the ideas of the Scriptures that we're trying to memorize, many times God breathes them again, into us, to transform us into His image. When we read the Bible, we gain some measure of understanding of the Bible. Then, when we pray the Bible, God breathes the thoughts of the Scriptures we are praying into our hearts so that we actually become the ideas of those Scriptures.

, , , , ,

From the Bible we discover God's great vision for us, our families, our cities, our nation, and our world.

, , , , ,

You have heard people say that we are the only Bible some people will ever read. This is true. And we know that we are sanctified by the Word of God. One major way this happens is when God breathes His Word into our hearts so that we're not just intellectually persuaded by the Scriptures, but we're internally transformed by the Scriptures. Then the Word of God is living and active in us.

Remember: the Bible is the basis of authority in all of life.

PRAY IN THE SPIRIT

Throughout the centuries, volumes have been written about the effectiveness of prayer that is dominated by the Holy Spirit. In a brief description of his own prayer life, Paul revealed in 1 Corinthians 14:14–15 two ways of praying: with the mind and with the spirit.

Praying with his mind means that he was praying in his native language or at least in a language that he understood with his natural mind. These are the prayers commonly spoken in group meetings in the church or before a meal. When praying in an understood language, we trust that our prayers are highly influenced by the Holy Spirit and that praying in a known language can be "praying in the spirit."

Paul also identifies prayer in another language, or "tongues." In 1 Corinthians 14:2 he writes, "For anyone who speaks in a tongue does not speak to men but to God. Indeed, no one understands him; he utters mysteries with his spirit." I believe tongues, then, are a way believers may pray in a language that they have not learned naturally.

Millions of believers worldwide have experienced praying in tongues. From 1 Corinthians 13:1, where Paul notes, "If I speak in the tongues of men and of angels," we can conclude that when people pray in tongues their spirits may be speaking to God in an earthly language from some other place or time, or they may be speaking in an angelic language. Either way, when believers pray this way, they edify themselves (1 Cor. 14:4), their prayers are the perfect will of God (Rom. 8:27), and their faith is strengthened (Jude 20).

❯ ❯ ❯ ❯ ❯

**Faults in character will give the devil a "place"
in your life that he will use to destroy your ability
to fulfill your primary purpose.**

❯ ❯ ❯ ❯ ❯

Why should people pray in tongues? The Book of Romans suggests that the Holy Spirit helps us express ourselves to God.

> In the same way, the Spirit helps us in our weakness. We do not know what we ought to pray for, but the Spirit himself intercedes for us with groans that words cannot express. And he who searches our hearts knows the mind of the Spirit, because the Spirit intercedes for the saints in accordance with God's will.
> —ROMANS 8:26–27

Praying in tongues is biblical but is not an end in itself; its purpose is to edify the believer so the believer can serve others.

GIVING THE DEVIL A FOOTHOLD

Throughout this chapter I have talked about how putting on the armor is living a lifestyle of character, and that character denies the devil a foothold in our lives. That principle comes from a key passage in Ephesians 4:27: "Neither give place to the devil" (KJV). This passage in Ephesians is surrounded with practical teaching about character, such as speaking the truth, controlling anger, earning a living, fleeing from sexual sin, and avoiding drunkenness.

Faults in character will give the devil a "place" in your life that he will use to destroy your ability to fulfill your primary purpose. It doesn't matter how spiritual you seem to other people. You won't fool the devil, and you won't fool God.

Remember: character counts.

—Fourteen—

Praying From Heaven

(Power Point #6)

W HEN RONALD REAGAN was an actor living in California, Communist leaders had no fear of his views, even though the actor had strong opinions about the threat Communist countries posed to the free world.

Then Reagan, the actor, became Reagan, the president of the United States. As president, he jokingly tested a microphone one day by saying, "Five, four, three, two, one—we just bombed Moscow." Those words caused a major international uproar. Not because Ronald Reagan the ex-actor said them, but because Reagan, the president of the United States, the one man on Earth in a position to initiate a major nuclear attack on the Soviet Union, had said them.

POSITION

The positions we hold indicate the authority we can exercise. After the "We just bombed Moscow" incident with the president, I was at church testing one of our new microphones, and I jokingly said, "Five, four, three, two, one—we just bombed Moscow." Absolutely no one cared. No bombers took off. NORAD didn't heighten its alert status. Ambassadors in Washington and Moscow weren't alarmed. Why? Because it didn't matter what I said. I didn't hold any political or military position. I wasn't the president.

Understanding our position is vital. A nineteen-year-old young man becomes a representative of his nation when he puts on the uniform of his country's armed services. He is still the same young man, but the uniform indicates his position. The man may enjoy certain freedoms and liberties as a citizen, but when he is in his uniform, his behavior must reflect a different standard—because of his position.

, , , , ,

When we became Christians, our position changed to one of being at the right hand of God, in Christ Jesus, co-laboring in His kingdom.

, , , , ,

We believers are required to embrace our position in Christ if we expect to become successful in prayer and action for our cities. I remind myself: always pray from heaven, never from Earth. Let me explain what I mean by "praying from heaven."

OUR POSITION IN CHRIST

In the beginning verses of Ephesians 2, Paul talks about the remarkable changes that have occurred in all who believe.

As nonbelievers, we were slaves to sin, bound by the world and victimized by the "ruler of the kingdom of the air, the spirit who is now at work in those who are disobedient" (v. 2). Then in verse 6 he says, "And God raised us up with Christ and seated us with him in the heavenly realms in Christ Jesus."

So when we became Christians, our position changed to one of being at the right hand of God, in Christ Jesus, co-laboring in His kingdom. We were no longer under the authority of evil spirits on Earth.

When I pray against demonic strategies, I must fully understand the reality of my position in Christ.

PERSONAL DEMONIC STRATEGIES

During the summer after my freshman year of college, I went home to Yorktown, Indiana, to spend the summer with my family and friends. One evening I went to Yorktown Baptist Church, the church instrumental in leading me to Christ, and entered the empty auditorium to pray.

No one else was in the building, so I was just relaxing and walking around casually fellowshiping with the Lord when I felt as if I were seeing something unusual. Since I had heard about people having visions in the Bible, I knew they happened during times of prayer, so I sat down in one of the empty chairs and continued praying.

I saw a delivery room where hospital personnel would bring women who were having their babies. Hovering over the delivery table, I saw a series of dark spirits of various sizes and shapes. One seemed to be in charge, and the others were waiting for his command.

As women were brought into the delivery room to give birth, the lead demon would assign one of the subordinate demons to each newborn baby. To one he would assign alcoholism; to another, sexual perversion; to another, religious arrogance; to another, the distraction of wealth or power. Some babies were assigned demons who would entice them toward fear, greed, hatred, self-consciousness, confusion, rebellion, or foolishness. As a nurse carried the baby and the mother was wheeled out, the demon assigned to the baby would accompany them.

From that vision I thought I gained insight into the seriousness of the devil's schemes. I could immediately identify in my own life the probable scheme the enemy would like to use to prevent me from achieving God's best for my life. I wanted to test the validity of my conclusion, so I also asked other people, "Can you tell me the one primary way the enemy would like to destroy you?" In practically every case the person questioned gave me a specific, immediate response.

Throughout life, people have opportunities to succumb to a variety of temptations, at times even encouraged by demonic forces. Though I believe that Satan uses specific demons to tempt individuals, that fact is not an excuse to give in to temptation. Demonic schemes must be resisted just as temptations that come from the flesh are resisted.

So how do we resist? Refuse to surrender your mind to sinful thoughts, refuse to act on sinful desires, and welcome the Holy Spirit into your life.

Prayer is also a powerful weapon against demonic schemes in a person's life. One who is not the recipient of Christian prayer may be unduly influenced by demons of hatred, lust, greed, self-pity, deceit, pride, and so on.

, , , , ,

Though I believe that Satan uses specific demons to tempt individuals, that fact is not an excuse to give in to temptation. Demonic schemes must be resisted just as temptations that come from the flesh are resisted.

, , , , ,

I believe these demonic spirits linger, waiting for an opportunity to become directly involved in a person's life. Should that person give them a foothold and learn to cooperate with them, the person may become demonized.

NEGATIVE COMMUNITY TRENDS

Just as demons have wicked plans for individuals, I believe more powerful ones have assignments to infect entire communities. If they thought about it, most Christians could describe the strategy that Satan uses to pollute their communities. What they may not realize is that these strategies are executed by evil spirits specializing in certain kinds of sin and deceit. For example, a city may be targeted by a spirit of lawlessness, occultism, greed, perversion, control, pride, poverty, etc.

The purpose of these spirits is to prevent the manifestations of God's kingdom, to paralyze Christians, and to promote their own evil nature through the lives of people within their territories.

According to Ephesians 1:21, Jesus has been given power over all "rule and authority, power and dominion, and every title that can be given, not only in the present age but also in the one to come." I am convinced this passage describes Jesus' authority over demonic spirits that desire to destroy people's lives. As we pray from our position in Christ, we too have authority over these demonic powers.

CHRISTIAN PRAYER STIMULATES THE HOLY SPIRIT'S ACTIVITY

I believe praying against this demonic activity unleashes an important spiritual dynamic. In praying for someone, our prayers always stimulate the Holy Spirit's activity in and around the person for whom we are praying. They also diminish the freedom of evil spirits that are hoping to gain additional influence over that person. Illustration 10 on page 160 demonstrates the change in a person's environment when he is the recipient of another's prayers.

As we pray for people, we have the authority to alter the spiritual atmosphere surrounding them. This authority does not include the ability to dominate their personal will—they are still responsible for their own choices. But if someone prays for them, their opportunities to receive positive spiritual input are greatly increased as demonic influences are displaced by the godly influences of either the Holy Spirit or angels. This means their potential to respond positively to the gospel greatly increases.

This is also an effective way to pray for leaders in society. For example, if we pray for the Senate, it obstructs the opportunities of evil spirits to suggest thoughts and ideas to our senators and facilitates the chance for the Holy Spirit to give them ideas. The same is true as we pray for Congress, the president, the police force, schoolteachers, pastors, and others.

This is also true when we pray for specific places. Praying for our cities can alter the spiritual climate as the removal of evil spirits makes way for God's blessing. The end result? A community on the receiving end of prayer has a much higher response to a gospel presentation than a community deprived of prayer. When effective Christian prayer is absent, the heavens are closed and demonic/worldly influences are dominant. But when Christians start praying, the demonic influences can become so weak that a vacuum actually develops, and

Illustration 10

The Impact of Prayer on an Individual

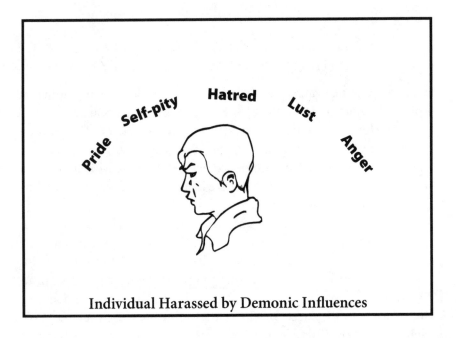

Individual Harassed by Demonic Influences

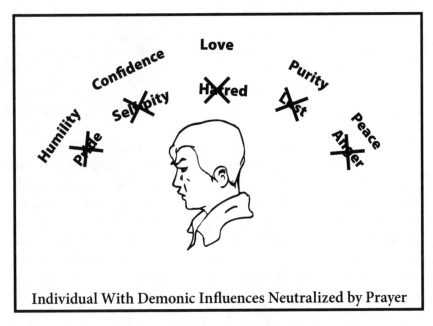

Individual With Demonic Influences Neutralized by Prayer

the kingdom of God can be manifested with greater effectiveness. In these places, massive conversions, life-giving church growth, societal improvement, and great spiritual encouragement occur. Illustration 11 on page 162 is a picture of a city's changing spiritual climate as believers pray.

, , , , ,

When effective Christian prayer is absent, the heavens are closed and demonic/worldly influences are dominant. But when Christians start praying, the demonic influences can become so weak that a vacuum actually develops, and the kingdom of God can be manifested with greater effectiveness.

, , , , ,

It's not hard. A little prayer goes a long way, and a lot of prayer does even more, stimulating the Holy Spirit's activity and thwarting demonic influence.

Christian prayer always diminishes the influence of demonic powers and stimulates the ministry of the Holy Spirit. It always works. It never fails. But we can't take any position on Earth and expect effectiveness. Instead we must pray from our position in heaven at the right hand of God in Christ Jesus, because only in Him do we have authority.

ALWAYS PRAY "FROM" HEAVEN

Paul drives this point home in Ephesians 3 when he writes, "His intent was that now, through the church, the manifold wisdom of God should be made known to the rulers and authorities in the heavenly realms, according to his eternal purpose which he accomplished in Christ Jesus our Lord" (vv. 10–11).

The world, the devil, and his demons do not want people to understand the realities of the gospel. The god of this world, Satan, works to blind the minds of those who don't believe. And no one can come to an understanding of the gospel unless the Holy Spirit reveals it supernaturally. Consequently, there is a massive spiritual struggle on the

Illustration 11

THE IMPACT OF PRAYER ON A CITY

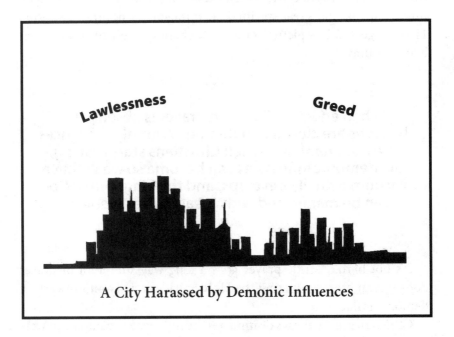

A City Harassed by Demonic Influences

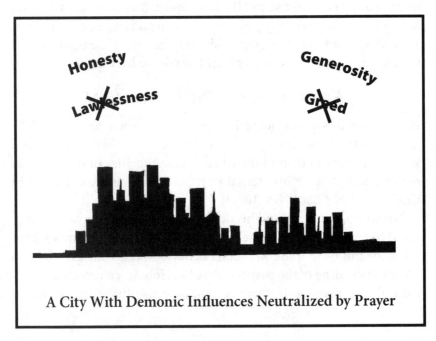

A City With Demonic Influences Neutralized by Prayer

enemy's part to keep people blinded to the gospel.

God has chosen, though, to use the church and believers to enforce the freedom available through the gospel. And that is the role of confrontational prayer. In prayer we gain life through communion with Him; then we use the position of authority in Jesus to make known the perfect will of God to demonic rulers and authorities. That's aggressive, confrontational prayer. It's not hard, it's not complex, nor is it mysterious. It always works when Christians do it. But it's not sweet—it's combat.

This is something only we in the church can do. There is no other group that can provide an environment of spiritual freedom that opens the door for people to respond to the gospel. Only we in the church, by praying from our position in heaven, can diminish demonic influences and stimulate the Holy Spirit's activity.

—FIFTEEN—

COMMUNING WITH GOD AND CONFRONTING THE ENEMY

(POWER POINT #7)

L ORD, I'M STARVING," I prayed one time after three days of prayer
and fasting. I was taking a walk through a forest in the foothills
of the Rockies and decided to tell God just how much I was suffering for Him.

"I am hungry for a Big Mac, a chicken leg, some corn or mashed
potatoes, and gravy," I moaned. "Please, God, I'm not playing any-
more. I may be dying. I want a chocolate shake, a loaf of bread, anything Chinese or Mexican. My pulse is rising, and my breathing is
shallow. I might not live much longer. This is the end. I have to have
some food."

After grumbling about my hunger some more, I smiled and said,
"Lord, I want You to know something. I'm really hungry for some
food—but I'm even more hungry for You."

I believe He smiled.

A DATE WITH GOD

I think of prayer and fasting as having a date with God. It is a specified
time set aside for me to spend time with Him and for Him to spend
time with me. I usually go for three days with a Bible, some juice and
water, a CD player and the Bible on CD, and great excitement.

When my friends ask me how to get started, I tell them to do a juice fast the first day, a water fast the second day, and juice again on the third day. I have found that keeps me alert, energetic, and sharp so I can walk, pray, study, or whatever I need to do while fasting. You might not enjoy it too much while you're fasting, but the results will be worth it when you are finished. In time, you can do water on all three days.

As you seek the Lord, abandon yourself in prayer. Pray until you press past your personal concerns and become consumed in His power. Push through your personal suffering into His suffering. Pray and fast for three days, and you will receive new ideas, refreshment, liberation, and strength. Then prepare for spiritual victory.

While praying and fasting, the enemy will try to perform every trick to paralyze you. He will try to trick you into excessive analysis or suggest that negative spiritual developments should be blamed on someone else. He will do all he can to distract you or cause you to fail. So keep it simple. Fast, pray, read your Bible, and let the Lord work in your life.

As you do that, God will give you ideas to help you manage your time, reorganize your priorities, eliminate your secret sins, conquer distractions in your life, and rethink failure and success. He will give you the wisdom necessary to keep you out of church politics and focused on purpose. He will teach you about rejection, hurt, passion, family, and finances. In the atmosphere of prayer and fasting, God will work miracles in your body, mind, and spirit.

, , , , ,

As you seek the Lord, abandon yourself in prayer. Pray until you press past your personal concerns and become consumed in His power.

, , , , ,

I try to fast three days every season (fall, winter, spring, and summer). I often invite several staff members to join me in prayer and fasting for those three days. We spend our days in individual prayer and communion and our evenings in corporate prayer and fellowship.

As we enjoy fellowship together in our hotel room, lodge, or tent, we talk about how fantastic it would be to have a cheeseburger, an extra large pepperoni pizza, or the largest banana split ever created. But our conversation always returns to the core idea that we desire God more than anything else.

Other times, I will retreat alone. I spend my time asking God to work His nature and Word into my heart and life. This process includes soaking in God's Word by listening to it on tape or CD, or sometimes watching videos depicting Scripture (the life of Moses, Paul, Jesus, etc.). It also obviously includes long talks with God. As I pray, people and situations come to mind, and God's forgiveness and insight flow into my heart, bringing life and healing. Regardless of how I spend my time fasting, each experience is a powerful, life-changing encounter with God.

I need to note, though, that typically I don't feel blessed while fasting. Actually, I hate it. But every time, I receive the reward after the time of prayer and fasting. Actually, the reward is so dramatic that I equate prayer and fasting to pouring jet fuel into a lawn mower. Prayer and fasting speed up God's work in our lives. We mature faster, grow faster, learn more, gain insight, and feel better. Prayer and fasting are incredibly powerful and invigorating—afterward, that is.

While praying and fasting, we become more spiritually sensitive— to both types of spiritual activity. As you commune with God, you can become saturated in Scripture, fellowship with the Holy Spirit, put off the flesh, and confront demonic activity. In that environment the absolutes of Scripture come alive. When our spirits are active, the absolutes are well defined. While praying and fasting, I enjoy praying the ideas from key scriptures. As I think about the scriptures, say them, and pray them, they come alive and become revelation in my heart, empowering me in dramatic ways.

While praying and fasting, God will give you thoughts on how to minister His Word to people not usually exposed to the gospel. Your intellect will become increasingly available to the Spirit, so ideas will flow freely as you seek the Lord and pray for those in your city. In this setting, ask God for a revelation of His love for the lost of your city. Ask Him to show you heaven and hell. Read the Scriptures regarding eternal life and eternal destiny.

And let His transformation take place. Let the love of Christ compel you and the fear of the Lord motivate you. Embrace the necessity of raising the water level of the Holy Spirit's activity. Pray that life-giving churches will grow, and new ones will be planted so thousands may come to Him. Pray for this process in your city so that strong, stable believers and life-giving local churches serve the people of your city.

,,,,,

I equate prayer and fasting to pouring jet fuel into a lawn mower. Prayer and fasting speed up God's work in our lives. We mature faster, grow faster, learn more, gain insight, and feel better.

,,,,,

In order to stay alert, I sometimes go on prayer walks through communities while praying and fasting. Other times I spend the hours seeking the Lord and listening to Scripture CDs. Fasting is a catalyst that the Holy Spirit uses to do a quick work in our lives. I believe the ministry of the Holy Spirit and the message of the Bible come alive during such times. Praying and fasting increase my spiritual authority, create humility, provide rich opportunity for personal spiritual warfare, and allow time for rest. This is constructive solitude—time to think.

I have never known one person with an addictive behavior who has been permanently set free without developing a lifestyle of prayer and fasting. The same character qualities are necessary to pray and fast that are required to live a life pleasing to the Lord. I think this is why the old preachers used to say, "He who prays, stays. And he who fasts, lasts."

We have a choice. We can learn to discipline our bodies and live a Spirit-filled life privately, while in the seclusion of prayer and fasting, or let the Lord teach us those lessons in public, which may be embarrassing. I choose prayer and fasting. This is where I want to learn about communion with God—knowing Him—and confrontation—denying the flesh and standing firm against the enemy's schemes.

In Luke 4, the Bible records Jesus' forty-day fast. During that time He obviously had tremendous encounters with God the Father, but He also had at least three major confrontations with the devil.

That is exactly the nature of our prayer times—both when we are fasting and when we are not. I believe that about 85 percent of our time in prayer should be spent fellowshiping with the Holy Spirit, communing with the Father in Jesus' name, praising and worshiping Him, and getting to know Him. Conversation with Him, knowing Him, and communicating with Him are the essence of our lives in Christ.

But that is not all of it. We also need to confront the enemy and his schemes. In the midst of confrontation we may verbally combat the enemy using the name of Jesus or specific Scripture verses. Confrontation is a vital part of what we do in prayer.

CONFRONTATION

Personal freedom and victory through communion and confrontation

"Pastor Ted, I need you to pray for me," Mrs. Grayson said with concern in her voice. "My family is in trouble because my little girl is out of control." She told me the story of her nine-year-old daughter, Susan*, who had been on medication for several years and was having to spend more and more time in the hospital. There was no consensus among her doctors about her specific diagnosis, but her mother was sure that schizophrenia was her illness.

"My daughter is so unpredictable. She seems so nice, but then she becomes so aggressive. What can we do? We don't want to lose our daughter!"

As she sat in my office crying, I asked her a number of questions trying to determine if the daughter's problem was indeed a mental illness or if she was struggling against evil spirits.

After our conversation the mother decided that she herself needed prayer. I agreed and offered to pray for her right then. She wanted deliverance.

---

* Names and details used in this story have been changed to protect the privacy of those involved.

As I prayed for her, she sat calmly with her eyes closed and her hands folded. Nothing seemed to be happening. After we finished, she thanked me cordially, and we walked together into the reception area.

The church secretary was anxiously waiting for us. She said Mrs. Grayson's husband had called several times but finally decided he couldn't wait for a return phone call. He was on his way to the church right then with Susan.

Mr. Grayson, like his wife, seemed very composed. Their daughter was pleasant. After all three came into my office, Mr. Grayson said, "Susan went into a trance about an hour ago and started saying things that didn't make any sense at all. She would say, 'Don't pray that. I hate you,' or 'I don't care what you say. I'm not coming out.' Another time she said, 'You are wicked. This is where we've lived for years, and you aren't going to make us move.'"

As he told us what she said, Mrs. Grayson and I both realized that Susan was responding to the prayer I had just prayed over her mother. I had never heard of such a thing.

I asked Susan if she would work with us in prayer to see if the Lord would heal her mother and her. She looked at me with hope in her eyes and agreed.

Over the next few months this family learned spiritual warfare. I gave them my warfare prayer book, *Simple Prayers for a Powerful Life*, so they would have enough information to pray effectively at home. They came to the office weekly, and we prayed and counseled together for an hour or so. After a few months, Susan no longer needed any hospital care, and her doctor was experimenting with reduced medication. After six months Susan was off her medication, enrolled in school, and becoming involved in church.

The same freedom that Susan experienced is available for all of us as we commune with the Lord and confront the schemes of the enemy. As a youth pastor years ago, I could easily distinguish the students whose parents regularly prayed for them and confronted demonic schemes from those whose parents did not. It was as if God placed a protective bubble around the students whose parents prayed for them regularly. That protection enabled those students to resist peer pressure, temptation, and demonic schemes more easily than the students whose parents did not pray. As parents spent time seeking the presence the Lord and confronting the schemes of the enemy, the Spirit of God would minister life and strength to their students and help them live in faith and victory.

, , , , ,

Each of us has the responsibility as believers to ensure that the people around us are able to live daily in the freedom and victory that Jesus has already provided.

, , , , ,

The Scriptures authorize us to liberate captives (Isa. 42:7; 49:9; 61:1), but too often we want to believe that we can do God's work without confrontation. I don't believe the biblical model of ministry allows us that luxury.

Each of us has the responsibility as believers to ensure that the people around us are able to live daily in the freedom and victory that Jesus has already provided. We do this through what we call "confronting the enemy." Confrontation helps to free us from the power of dark thoughts and negative spiritual and emotional ties so we can soar into freedom in Christ.

I believe deliverance ministry is so important that it is the responsibility of every Christian to know how to cast a demon out of a demonized person. (If you feel as if you don't know how to cast out a demon, look at the examples Jesus gave in the Gospel of Mark.)

We also have the responsibility to confront demonic activity on the occult level. Occult-level warfare negates demonic activity stimulated through the occult. For example, spiritual warfare on the occult level would be needed in a situation where an occult curse brought demonic attacks into a person's life. I also believe we can pray against demonic schemes that often come against church bodies as a whole.

Practically every Saturday night when I go to the church to pray for the upcoming Sunday services, I pray to cancel the spiritual power of any negative words or actions that have been launched against our church body, the families of our church, and my family in particular. I also pray that God will send angels as ministering spirits to minister to every individual as an heir of salvation as they walk through the doors of our church.

I believe individuals, families, and churches should regularly pray for freedom from occult bondage because there is no way to know what others are trying to do to you spiritually.

Regional freedom and victory through communion and confrontation

We also must confront demonic powers that influence entire regions. These are strategic prayers that every believer must be prepared to pray.

When we pray for a region, we assume our position in Christ at the right hand of the Father and use that authority to pray for the spiritual climate of the entire region. That type of praying is effective anytime at weakening demonic principalities and blessing people.

Sometimes we travel to key locations or places of spiritual power in order to pray on site. High places overlooking a city or spiritual power points in a city are effective spots to pray strategically against spirits that impact groups of people, similar to the way the prince of Persia exercised authority in Daniel 10. I consider power points to be places where demonically manipulated people go to do things that will strengthen the demonic activities in a region, like a particularly popular bar, cult-type church, or occult worship site. Very often these are high points overlooking a large area. Sometimes particular government buildings, Masonic lodges, or old religious sites are also power points.

In October 1993 I led a team of thirty-one people on a prayer journey to pray strategically for Albania. While there we had three vivid experiences in which members of our team experienced strategic-level spiritual warfare. One of those occurred when I accompanied three others to a cave in the side of a mountain where a local Islamic boy had told us demonic activity was taking place.

Fifteen hundred years earlier a man went to the top of this mountain to pray because he was so burdened by his sin. While praying, he realized that he needed atonement. This grieved him terribly. In the midst of his sin and because of his lack of knowledge, he entered a large cave in the side of the mountain and killed himself, hoping to make atonement for his own sinfulness.

That cave has been a place of animal (and maybe human) sacrifice ever since.

, , , , ,

We have a choice. We can learn to discipline our bodies and live a Spirit-filled life privately, while in the seclusion of prayer and fasting, or let the Lord teach us those lessons in public, which may be embarrassing.

, , , , ,

Our guide led us to the narrow stairway built into the face of the cliff leading to the cave. We saw drops of fresh blood shimmering on the stone steps. The guide was so frightened as we neared the entrance of the cave that, as soon as he had pointed out the place we were looking for, he took off. The rest of us realized that this high place had become an evil stronghold centuries earlier and we had to do all we could to neutralize the demonic activity.

As we walked down into the cave, we noticed a pair of shoes at the entrance, characteristic of a place of worship in Eastern countries. Because of the shoes, we realized that one of the worshipers was still present from the morning sacrifice. Upon entering the worship area, we noted Islamic religious symbols distorted by their makers into satanic symbols. (I had seen the same type of distortions in American Satanism, except that in America they use Christian or Jewish symbols and distort them.)

As we walked and confronted demons in the name of Jesus, we came to a dark cavern with dozens of candles on the floor and ledges. In fervent confrontational prayer we prayed that only the God of Israel—the God of Abraham, Isaac, and Jacob—would be worshiped in this place. We took oil, a symbol of the Holy Spirit's ministry, and placed it on the candles and on the walls darkened by hundreds of years of smoke.

As we prayed, we sensed that waves of freedom were pouring into the cave, but we felt we should press on to find the place of sacrifice.

With our adrenaline flowing and our senses alert because of the unusual combination of fear and confidence, we passed through the worship area to see another branch of the cave that went even deeper into the mountain. Upon entering we saw four covered altars and, just beyond them, an underground spring. We immediately felt great fear and waves of terror. We were praying, thinking, worrying—and nervously watching for the worshiper we thought was probably hiding in a crevice somewhere.

We confronted terror with confidence in being His ambassadors. We overcame anxiety from the obvious danger with thoughts of serving people by liberating them from demonic religious manipulation. Fear came and went. But faith was always there.

We started breaking curses, anointing altars with oil, driving demons out of the cave, and asking God's glory to fill the place in Jesus' name. A couple of the team members stayed near the entrance and prayed for our protection. We realized that God was doing a great miracle.

As terror subsided and confidence increased, we left the cave wondering why we never located the owner of the shoes at the entrance. By now the blood was dry on the steps. As we walked away from the cave, we saw a group of nationals who had gathered at the top of the mountain and were running about and yelling. They were telling people excitedly that a group of Americans had come to drive the demons away from the cave.

In the midst of joy and excitement, though, at the pinnacle of the mountain stood a small woman in a black dress, pointing at us with one hand and spinning her demonic prayer wheel with the other. We saw her and began praying for her and walking toward her. She ran away from us toward a wooded area while continuing to spin her prayer wheel.

While two of us diverted the attention of the nationals who had gathered, a couple of the ladies who were with us went to the top of the hill and prayed for God's blessing and mercy to come upon the people of this region. That is strategic-level spiritual warfare.

How do we know the prayer journey to Albania was effective? According to reports we received from numerous sources, the body of Christ there grew 600 percent from October 1993 to October 1994. There were many reasons for that growth, and the size of the body of Christ in Albania is still unacceptably small. But Albanians now willing to accept the gospel is one indicator that prayer has been, and continues to be, effective.

As you pray, it is important to consider what dark spiritual activity may be trying to hinder the growth of God's kingdom. Very simply, use the authority you have in Christ to weaken or remove those demonic principalities. In your hometown, that prayer is prayed two ways:

1. Through verbally confronting demonic activity and praying for God's kingdom to be established

2. By a lifestyle that expresses your faith

THY KINGDOM COME

Obviously, the manifestation of the kingdom of God in people's lives must be the desired result of all intercession. Before and after times of spiritual confrontation, communion with the Father is very necessary. Often I pray the portion of the Lord's prayer that says, "Your kingdom come, your will be done on earth as it is in heaven" (Matt. 6:10).

God wants to bless His people. Two familiar Scriptures remind us of this. In Numbers 6:24–25 the Bible says, "The LORD bless you and keep you; the LORD make his face shine upon you and be gracious to you; the LORD turn his face toward you and give you peace." This is God's blessing for us. We don't have to talk Him into it. We simply have to receive it. Another that comes to mind is the famous prayer of Jabez in 1 Chronicles 4:10: "Jabez cried out to the God of Israel, 'Oh, that you would bless me and enlarge my territory! Let your hand be with me, and keep me from harm so that I will be free from pain.' And

God granted his request." God's desire is to pour His blessing and His life into the darkness of the earth. He doesn't resist it, so when we commune with Him, He quickly responds.

Praying for God's kingdom to come and His will to be done on Earth as it is in heaven is particularly powerful in praying for lost people. When we pray for God's kingdom to be established in people's hearts, we are asking that His Spirit work in their lives.

I take three primary lists from the Bible—the characteristics of the Holy Spirit (Isa. 11:2), the fruit of the Spirit (Gal. 5:22–23), and the gifts of the Spirit (1 Cor. 12:7–10)—and pray that they will be manifested in the lives of people. I know that the fruit and the gifts can only be fully manifested in the lives of believers. But they are also blessings in nonbelievers' lives to whatever degree they can influence. I believe that God is sovereign, and that we—as ambassadors, co-laborers, and members of His body—are here to fulfill His plan. If God can prophesy through a donkey, He can certainly work through people who haven't formally submitted to Him. So, I pray for everyone to be blessed and used by God, no matter their understanding of the spiritual world.

, , , , ,

When we pray for God's kingdom to be established in people's hearts, we are asking that His Spirit work in their lives.

, , , , ,

When praying for others, ask God to give them these blessings. Taking the time to study each of these subjects will enhance your fervency as you pray, "Your kingdom come, your will be done on earth as it is in heaven." These are the evidences of the kingdom of God in people. Pray that God will give them:

Isaiah 11:2

- The Spirit of the Lord
- The Spirit of wisdom
- The Spirit of understanding

- The Spirit of counsel
- The Spirit of power
- The Spirit of knowledge
- The Spirit of the fear of the Lord

Galatians 5:22–23

- Love
- Joy
- Peace
- Patience
- Kindness
- Goodness
- Faithfulness
- Gentleness
- Self-control

1 Corinthians 12:7–10

- Message of wisdom
- Message of knowledge
- Faith
- Gifts of healing
- Miraculous powers
- Prophecy
- Distinguishing between spirits
- Tongues
- Interpretation of tongues

As you are praying, look over these lists and ask God to give His Spirit to you and to others. Ask for "the Spirit of the fear of the Lord" to minister. Pray for God to send self-control and faithfulness to people. Think of the results when you pray for the Spirit of prophecy to come upon government officials or the message of wisdom to work through judges and juries. Pray for every police officer to distinguish between spirits. (I believe simply praying for Colorado Springs police officers has contributed to the increased effectiveness of our police department.)

We pray that God will give every citizen faith. Their increased confidence in God because of faith will prepare them to receive the gospel. We need healing in our hearts, miraculous powers to protect our children, and goodness and faithfulness in every home.

"Your kingdom come, your will be done on earth as it is in heaven."

Everything on these lists is evidence of His kingdom. Everything on these lists is His perfect will. Everything on these lists allows a little slice of heaven on earth.

PRAYER AND ACTION

Very often people ask me how to mobilize prayer in their local churches. I encourage them to:

1. Be a person of prayer. Don't just promote prayer; pray.

2. Have symbols of prayer around your church. At New Life we have a 15-foot globe in our prayer center to remind us of the needs of people around the world. We also use other reminders to help people remember the importance of prayer, such as keeping the Communion elements readily available and using large plasma screens to display the world prayer team Web site (www.worldprayerteam.org) so people can pray for prayer requests from around the world.

3. Lead prayer journeys. When people walk and pray through key sites in another city, they become attached to that city for evangelism and the growth of the church. Right now we're concerned about key sections of Pakistan, northern India, the area around Israel, Iran, Iraq, Lebanon, North Korea, and Cuba. As a result, we're sending prayer teams into these countries. Is it dangerous? Yes. Sometimes we will just have the team get as close as possible without getting into unreasonable danger in order to pray. Other times we will have a team go to a retreat facility with maps and information about the country they are praying for and pray from there. But some in the church will want to actually go to the danger area, and we let them. It's powerful, both for missions efforts and for other work on the ground in those countries.

4. After people have gone on a prayer journey, they are so concerned for that area they will want to fund Christian activities in that region. As a result, we identify Christian works in every region where we send prayer teams so we can follow up in a practical way. When prayer is combined with action to promote the gospel, tangible results always follow.

This is all prayer. Saying prayers and doing prayers go hand in hand.

—CONCLUSION—

HEAVEN OR HELL? OUR GENERATION. OUR CHOICE.

ETERNITY IS FINAL. The Scriptures give only one guaranteed way for any human being to spend eternity in heaven: Jesus Christ. Even some evangelicals try to avoid the finality of eternal judgment and the realities of heaven and hell; nonetheless, these are the facts: heaven or hell for every person…forever. No recourse.

I don't value pastoring a big church, having big budgets, or having best-selling books. I love simple living. I would be more satisfied pastoring a small church of two hundred or so somewhere in the Midwest. I wouldn't mind living in an older house with a front porch and a sidewalk so that Gayle and I and the kids could sit on the porch in the evenings and greet people as they walk by. It's my dream to sell hot dogs at the Friday night football games while living in a town small enough to know the football players' parents, aunts, uncles, cousins, and nephews.

But none of these things will ever be in my life. Why? Because I'm obsessed with the reality and finality of heaven and hell. No doubt, there are many who are legitimately called to serve Christ in small settings, but I can't. I need to be where we can reach lots of people, fund lots of missionaries, and maximize discipleship.

This is our generation. It doesn't belong to anyone else. We are the church of this generation. There is no other. If we do a good job, the future will be better for all of mankind. If we do a bad job, should Christ tarry, it could take hundreds, if not thousands of years for another generation to have the opportunities that we have had in this one. We have no choice. We must be faithful. We must be emptied of ourselves, our own desires, wants, opinions, and concerns, and we must be consumed by the passions of Jesus. He paid an incredible price and has strategically positioned us so that we can reach every person on the globe. Nothing or no one can stop us except...us. If we are distracted, selfish, greedy, narrow, ill informed, or spiritually weak, we will miss this opportunity. If we will focus and do what we know to do, we will achieve the task He has given us. All of Christian history can culminate here if we will be diligent.

But I'm not encouraged. Too many of our evangelical seminary leaders don't pray and fast, memorize the Scriptures, or pray in the Spirit. Too many of them would rather debate the meaning of being Spirit-filled than seek God earnestly in order to be Spirit-filled. Too many of our millionaires lead or invest in Christian ministries but haven't given their all to reach the lost, help the poor, or rescue the perishing. They tip enough to demonstrate that they believe, but most don't give so deeply that it affects their lifestyles. I know of many Christian authors who are rich and famous, and they spend their money in the same ways that worldly people do—big houses, cars, and investments. We're fat. Too many pastors think the church is about them; too many board members think their role is to control and protect instead of empower. God's heart is broken. Judgment day will not be what many of us hope for.

Now, we may be doing better than we've ever done. But there are also more unreached than ever before, more Muslims than ever before, more secularists than ever before, and more atheists than ever before. Even though we are doing better than ever, because of the global population explosion, we also have greater needs and greater opportunity than ever.

There are two motivations that must work within every one of us. One is the love of Christ that compels us. The other is the terror of the Lord that consumes us and requires that we tell others about Him.

Because of this reality, for years I distributed the obituaries from the morning paper to every staff member at New Life Church. On the obituaries I would place a sticky-note that read:

Today from Colorado Springs people will go to heaven, and people will go to hell. The percentage of people going to heaven and the percentage of people going to hell today is determined by how well you did your job yesterday. If you remember heaven today, it will help someone else avoid hell tomorrow.

Why did I do this? Because we all need to be reminded constantly of our primary purpose: to make it hard to go to hell from our generation. This is all we do.

The Bible provides a clear picture of hell. Jesus had an intense concern that people avoid hell because it is where "the worm does not die, and the fire is not quenched" (Mark 9:48). When Jesus referred to hell, He often would describe it as Gehenna, which was a burning dump near Jerusalem. That's a metaphor for one potential eternal destination: perpetual burning with worms, maggots, fire, remorse and torment, agonized wailing, the painful grinding of teeth, and the endless sizzling of burning human flesh, separated from God's goodness and grace.

Alone.

No way out.

No second chance.

God does not want anyone to spend eternity in hell (2 Pet. 3:9). Hell was prepared for the devil and his demons (Matt. 25:41), so the only people that perish are those who reject God. God doesn't send them to hell; they send themselves by choice (John 3:17–18).

THE CHURCH

As I mentioned earlier, the apostle Paul lists two major motivations for his effective ministry. One is found in 2 Corinthians 5:11, where he writes, "Knowing therefore the terror of the Lord, we persuade men" (KJV). This passage reveals that Paul had a sincere understanding of the horrible nature of the wrath of God and the terror that will come upon His enemies. Therefore, he feared for those who did not know the gospel. Paul was consumed with the finality of that reality and, therefore, was motivated to persuade men.

A few verses later Paul writes, "For Christ's love compels us" (2 Cor. 5:14). Then he gives an explanation of the gospel. Here he communicates that he is compelled by the love of Christ for himself and for others. It seems as though Paul had a clear understanding of the reality that judgment is real but that God is deeply in love with mankind. The gospel, then, tells us that no man needs to pay the price for his own sins and that each one can avoid judgment by faith in Christ Jesus. God's wrath and God's love constrained Paul and determined the course of his life.

The responsibility of that message is now entrusted to you and me, the church.

- We are the only ones with the message that guarantees eternal life.

- We are the only ones with unlimited access to God the Father.

- We are the only ones with the power of the Holy Spirit and the authority to negate the influence of demonic strategies.

- We are the only ones who are able to overcome the gates of hell.

- We are the only ones with the global opportunities who can do His job.

- We are the only ones who are exclusively responsible because we are His body, His co-workers, His ambassadors, His friends.

- We understand the church.

- We understand spiritual power.

- We understand godly living.

- We can do this.

- We are responsible.

He gave us His nature, His will, His plan, His Spirit, His grace, His love, and His anointing.

Our role as liberators is a life-giving responsibility. Paul referred to this when he said, "I am clear of my responsibility. From now on I will go to the Gentiles" (Acts 18:6). He was referring to the fact that he had preached to the Jewish people in this region as he was responsible to do, but now that they had rejected the message, his responsibility required him to go to the Gentiles.

Now, before you look for the end of this chapter, pay particularly close attention to this point.

In Acts 20:26–27, Paul writes, "Therefore, I declare to you today that I am innocent of the blood of all men. For I have not hesitated to proclaim to you the whole will of God." In other words, if he hadn't preached, he would have been guilty of their blood. But since he did preach to them, he was relieved of the burden of their eternal plight.

He may have been thinking of the passage from Ezekiel 3:17–21, where God told Ezekiel:

> Son of man, I have made you a watchman for the house of Israel; so hear the word I speak and give them warning from me. When I say to a wicked man, "You will surely die," and you do not warn him or speak out to dissuade him from his evil ways in order to save his life, that wicked man will die for his sin, and I will hold you accountable for his blood. But if you do warn the wicked man and he does not turn from his wickedness or from his evil ways, he will die for his sin; but you will have saved yourself.
>
> Again, when a righteous man turns from his righteousness and does evil, and I put a stumbling block before him, he will die. Since you did not warn him, he will die for his sin. The righteous things he did will not be remembered, and I will hold you accountable for his blood. But if you do warn the righteous man not to sin and he does not sin, he will surely live because he took warning, and you will have saved yourself.

Do you see the idea? If we don't tell others, we will share the responsibility for their plight. If we do, then the responsibility falls on them.

As I mentioned in an earlier chapter, every year we at New Life Church put on an Easter production called "The Thorn: An Epic Encounter." This production started several years ago when our youth pastor at the time, John Bolin, wrote a short sketch for the kids to portray the story of the cross in a dramatic fashion. I walked in on one of these little plays and instantly knew that not only did our church body as a whole need to see this performance, but we also needed to show it to the community. Now, eight years later, the performance uses more than 1,000 volunteers, almost 10 percent of our church members. We don't take hundreds of hours of volunteer time and spend the tithes and offerings of our church for frivolity, fun, and games. This is not about entertainment. Last year more than 50,000 people saw "The Thorn." Now, even if every single member of our 12,000-person church saw it, that still means almost 40,000 people from our community saw a dramatic biblical account of the life, death, and resurrection of Jesus Christ.

Good work, but not good enough. There are now 500,000 people in our community.

This is life and death. We don't do it as a gimmick because we want to have one more event to bring our people together or grow our church body with transfers from other churches. We do it because we have no choice. We have to reach out. The blood is on our hands—Colorado Springs is our responsibility. As members of the body of Christ, we are the ones with the authority to remove demonic activity and stimulate the Holy Spirit's activity in the lives of the people of our city. We have the message that can save, heal, and bless their lives.

When we give all we can to missionaries, help plant other churches, train our young men and women to use every opportunity to reach others, put on "The Thorn," distribute Bibles all over our city, give out JESUS videos, do prayer walks, and treat others with the honor that Christ has for them, we do that for a purpose that only we can perform. We in the body are the only ones who can get people back to the tree of life. We are the only ones who can demonstrate that humility and respect overpower control and manipulation. The church has the power to have genuine character through the armor God gives us. We can commune with God and overcome enemy strongholds—and no one else can.

That's why the Scripture says, "If my people, who are called by my name, will humble themselves and pray and seek my face and turn from their wicked ways, then will I hear from heaven and will forgive their sin and will heal their land" (2 Chron. 7:14).

This verse clearly communicates that as we in the body do what only we can do, we set the stage for the healing of our land. That is the point of this entire book. We have the resources, the spiritual power, and the will of God. Only we can do what needs to be done—make it easy to go to heaven from our cities.

NOTES

CHAPTER 1
OUR PURPOSE, OUR OPPORTUNITY

1. Ted Haggard, *Primary Purpose* (Lake Mary, FL: Charisma House, 1995); Ted Haggard and Jack Hayford, *Loving Your City into the Kingdom* (Ventura, CA: Regal Books, 1997); John Dawson, *Taking Our Cities for God* (Lake Mary, FL: Charisma House, 1989); and Ed Silvoso, *That None Shall Perish* (Ventura, CA: Regal Books, 1994).

2. Philip Jenkins, "The Next Christianity," *Atlantic Monthly*, Vol. 290, No. 3, October 2002.

3. Andy Crouch, "The Cruel Edges of the World," *Christianity Today*, Vol. 48, No. 6, June 2004, 60.

Other Books and Booklets by Author

Books

The Life-Giving Church

Dog Training, Fly Fishing, and Sharing Christ in the 21st Century

Simple Prayers for a Powerful Life

Letters From Home

Loving Your City Into the Kingdom

Taking It to the Streets

Confident Parents, Exceptional Teens (with John Bolin)

Foolish No More!

The Jerusalem Diet

Booklets

Who's in Charge Here

So You Want to Get Married

No More Lonely Nights

Fraud in the Storehouse

How to Take Authority Over Your Mind, Home, Business and Country

Liberation Through Prayer and Fasting

Freedom Through Forgiveness

Free Enterprise

Teaching Series and Videos by Author

Teaching Series (CDs)

A Place to Worship

The S Series (Suicide, Sexual Purity, Suffering, Satan)

The Providence of God

Videos

Loving Your City Into the Kingdom

Prayerwalking Your City

Primary Purpose

To order these resources or for further information, contact:

New Life Church
11025 Voyager Parkway
Colorado Springs, CO 80921
Phone: (719) 594-6602

Web sites:
www.newlifechurch.org
www.tedhaggard.com